The Financial Technology Revolution

Turgay Geçer · Vedat Akgiray

The Financial Technology Revolution

Theory, Innovation, and Revenue Streams

palgrave
macmillan

Turgay Geçer
Department of Management
FSM Vakif University
Istanbul, Türkiye

Vedat Akgiray
Boğaziçi University
Istanbul, Türkiye

ISBN 978-3-031-92050-9 ISBN 978-3-031-92048-6 (eBook)
https://doi.org/10.1007/978-3-031-92048-6

This Palgrave Macmillan imprint is published by the registered company Springer Nature Switzerland AG
The registered company address is: Gewerbestrasse 11, 6330 Cham, Switzerland

CONTENTS

About the Authors

Turgay Geçer is an Associate Professor in the Department of Management at the Faculty of Economics and Administrative Sciences, FSM Vakif University, Istanbul. His primary research interests include FinTech, AI, banking, credit analysis, and risk management.

Vedat Akgiray is a professor of finance and director of the Center for Research in Finance at Boğaziçi University, Istanbul. His current research interest is in sustainable and ethical finance with a focus on financial technologies.

Abbreviations and Acronyms

3D	3 Domain
A2A	Account to Account
AI	Artificial Intelligence
AML	Anti Money Laundering
API	Application Programming Interface
ATM	Automated Teller Machine
B2B	Business to Business
B2P	Business to Person
BaaS	Banking as a Service
BIS	Bank for International Settlements
BNPL	Buy Now Pay Later
CBDC	Central Bank Digital Currencies
CeFi	Centralized Finance
CEX	Centralized Exchange
CTF	Counter-Terrorism Financing
DeFi	Decentralized Finance
DEX	Decentralized Exchange
DL	Deep Learning
dPOS	Digital POS
EMI	Equated Monthly Installments
EMV	Europay, MasterCard and Visa
EU	European Union
FX	Foreign Exchange
GSM	Global System for Mobile Communications
HSM	Hardware Security Module
HTML	Hypertext Markup Language

HTTP	Hypertext Transfer Protocol
IPO	Initial Public Offerings
ISO	International Organization for Standards
IT	Information Technology
KYC	Know Your Customer
LLM	Large Language Model
M2M	Me to Me
ML	Machine Learning
mPOS	Mobile POS
NFC	Near Field Communications
NLP	Natural Language Processing
P2B	Person to Business
P2P	Person to Person
PAN	Primary Account Number
PBOC	People's Bank of China
PC	Personal Computer
PCI DSS	Payment Card Industry Data Security Standard
PCI SSC	Payment Card Industry Security Standards Council
PIN	Personal Identification Number
POS	Point of Sale
PSD2	Payment Services Directive 2
PSD3	Payment Services Directive 3
PSP	Payment Service Provider
QR	Quick Response
RTO	Rent to Own
SCA	Strong Customer Authentication
SEC	Securities and Exchange Commission
SME	Small Medium Enterprise
sPOS	Soft POS
SRC	Secure Remote Commerce
SWIFT	Society for Worldwide Interbank Financial Telecommunication
TCP/IP	Transmission Control Protocol/Internet Protocol
TPP	Third-party Provider
TSP	Token Service Provider
UX/UI	User Experience/User Interface
vPOS	Virtual POS

List of Figures

List of Tables

List of Case Studies

CHAPTER 1

Introduction

Abstract This chapter provides a comprehensive analysis of FinTech and its transformative impact on financial services through technology. It examines key sectors such as payments, digital banking, investments, and insurance, highlighting how technological advances, evolving user expectations, and regulatory requirements are driving the rapid expansion of FinTech. The chapter traces the evolution of FinTech from beginning to maturity, addressing challenges such as securing funding, developing technology infrastructure, and ensuring regulatory compliance. It also examines the roles of traditional financial institutions and technology companies, illustrating how their collaboration is reshaping the finance industry. Finally, the chapter highlights the importance of innovation, agility, and compliance in achieving sustainable success in the highly competitive FinTech sector.

Keywords FinTech lifecycle · Seed stage · Early stage · Growth stage · Maturity stage

FinTech is a business model based on digitalized financial services. It includes technology-driven innovations that create new business models, platforms, processes, and products and have a significant impact on the delivery of financial services (FSB, 2019). FinTech is the result

T. Geçer and V. Akgiray, *The Financial Technology Revolution*,
https://doi.org/10.1007/978-3-031-92048-6_1

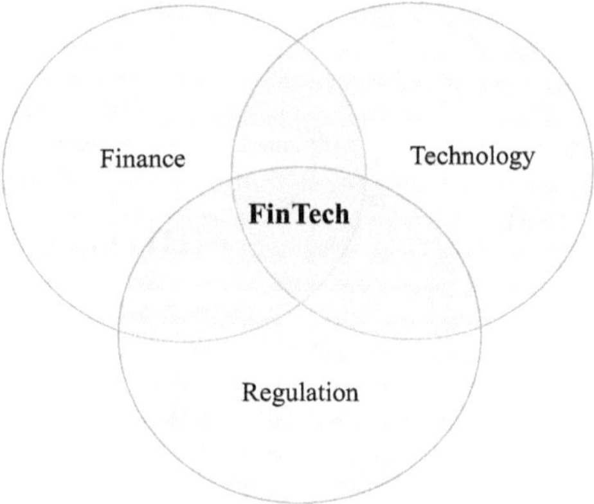

Fig. 1.1 Intersection of FinTech

of the evolution of technology and finance, transforming the financial industry by challenging traditional systems and enhancing financial products. Its rapid growth in recent years has been driven by technological advances, changing user expectations, increased funding, and stronger regulatory support (KPMG, 2017). Well-positioned at the intersection of finance, technology, and regulation, FinTech is remonetizing technology by reinterpreting financial services.

Figure 1.1 illustrates that FinTech is at the intersection of finance, technology, and regulation.

FinTech has the potential to revolutionize financial services in areas such as payments, market provisioning, asset management, insurance, deposits, lending, and capital raising (WEF, 2015). It is reinterpreting financial services through technology. The magic of FinTech is to transform complex technologies into less complex financial experiences. FinTech provides hyper-personalized, integrated digital solutions that increase accessibility and improve user engagement with financial services. This user-centric approach, combined with the speed and convenience of FinTech, is reshaping user preferences and driving transformative change in the financial industry (Saini, 2018). In addition, it offers cost-effective alternatives to conventional methods while ensuring compliance with international security standards. FinTech is an "**übersector**" that transcends traditional finance, creating value-added services that significantly impact banking, payments, and commerce.

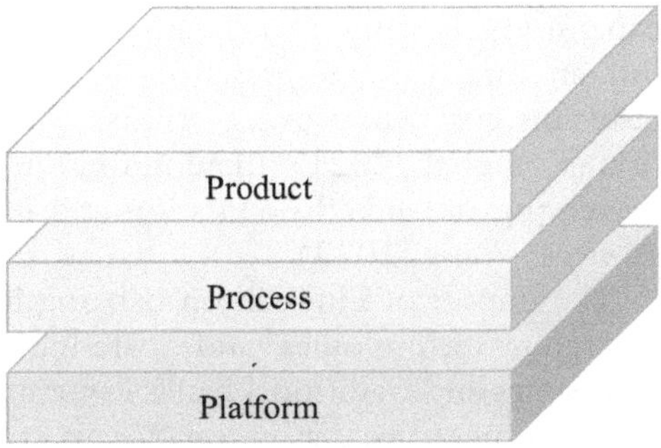

Fig. 1.2 Layers of FinTech

Figure 1.2 illustrates the interrelated and sequential layers of FinTech: platform, process, and product.

FinTech consists of three interconnected layers: platform, process, and product. Platform is the foundation of FinTech, such as payment, digital wallet, digital banking, investment, and insurance platforms. Process is the digitization through QR codes, AI, ML, DL, NLP, UX/UI, APIs, tokenization, and compliance and security measures. The product is the promise of value for money and unprecedented user experiences. Products include payment accounts, payment cards, loans, investments, and insurance services. These layers are tightly coupled, facilitating the integration of platforms and processes into products. This interdependence enhances flexibility, scalability, and adaptability, fostering continuous innovation and efficiency across financial ecosystem.

1.1 Formation of FinTech

1.1.1 FinTech by Financial Institutions

FinTech is a rapidly growing and highly publicized sector in the finance industry (Mercer Capital, 2018). Traditional banks and financial institutions benefit from FinTech in several ways. First, they can attract tech-savvy younger generations, such as Generations X and Z, by offering products tailored to their specific needs. This strategy diversifies revenue streams and increases market share. FinTech companies have disrupted the industry by introducing innovative products and services that increase user engagement and improve service quality. Second, to remain competitive, financial institutions must adapt to new technologies and evolving business models (KPMG, 2017). In addition, FinTech facilitates global expansion, allowing financial institutions to enter new markets and establish an international presence. It strengthens the financial system by reducing costs, improving service quality, and increasing user satisfaction (Kou et al., 2021). In addition, FinTech promotes financial inclusion by serving unbanked population and increasing access to basic financial services (Wang, 2023).

The impact of FinTech on banking industry is significant. Leveraging emerging technologies and fostering collaboration between FinTech companies and traditional banks can enhance financial stability while mitigating competitive disruption (Varma et al., 2022). To effectively navigate the rise of FinTech, financial institutions can adopt one of seven strategies: acquire FinTech companies, partner with them, invest in them, transform operations to adopt FinTech-like models, build internal FinTech capabilities, serve FinTech companies, or ignore them (McKinsey, 2024a). The most common approach among banks is to partner with FinTech companies or merger and acquisition (IMF, 2022).

1.1.2 FinTech by Technology Companies

Technology companies are increasingly investing in financial services, having established strong brand recognition and a broad user base. Their expansion into finance represents a natural extension of their core business, allowing them to leverage synergies between financial services and their existing businesses while benefiting from economies of scope and scale (BIS, 2019b).

Increasingly, technology companies recognize FinTech as a strategic growth opportunity that aligns with their long-term profitability goals. They are implementing two main strategies: strengthening and diversifying their core businesses (Tanda & Schena, 2019). Their ability to innovate and develop advanced technologies enables them to generate significant revenues in FinTech sector, while providing impeccable digital and financial services. Their business model is based on the monetization of information shared by users (Bethlendi & Szőcs, 2022). By integrating with FinTech solutions, these companies can attract new users while enhancing financial services for their existing ones. With large user databases, they have a competitive advantage over conventional banks and financial institutions, allowing them to offer more comprehensive and integrated services (Folwarski, 2020).

1.1.3 FinTech by Individuals or Companies

Individuals or companies can begin FinTech venture. Establishing a FinTech company to offer innovative financial products or develop new financial concepts presents a promising opportunity for both individuals and companies.

However, several key requirements must be met for successful establishment. First, an impeccable idea is essential to stand out in FinTech sector. Second, a comprehensive business model that outlines goals, strategies, market analysis, and financial projections must be developed. Third, securing funding is critical, with potential sources including personal savings, family, friends, or angel investors. In the early stages, investors are more likely to support a FinTech venture based on its story and potential rather than its financial performance. Developing innovative and high-quality FinTech products necessitates a robust technology infrastructure. Equally important are strong marketing skills, as entrepreneurs must effectively promote their concepts and identify their target users. Their ability to market their FinTech ideas is a key indicator of their marketing capabilities. Additionally, offering a unique value proposition is vital for differentiation in the FinTech arena. Collaborating with banks, financial institutions, technology companies, or other FinTech companies can create new business opportunities. In the highly regulated FinTech sector, comprehending and ensuring regulatory compliance is critical, as non-compliance can result in serious legal consequences. Furthermore, regulations can directly impact business models (Haddad & Hornuf, 2019).

1.2 Operating Cycles of FinTech

FinTech is a business model that digitalizes financial services by leveraging data and reinterpreting conventional financial products. By combining financial services with technology, FinTech company generates new data, develops innovative products, and drives financial industry transformation.

<u>Internal Cycle</u>

FinTech is a digital organism created in an entrepreneur's mind and living on servers. It begins with a brilliant idea to make financial services faster, more accessible, and affordable through technology. For new products to succeed, they must be backed by reliable information. Each product generates new data that drives a continuous cycle of development and refinement. This data-to-product-to-data cycle allows FinTech products to be continually evaluated and improved, fostering continuous innovation.

External Cycle

Key capability of many FinTech companies is their ability to collect and analyze vast amounts of data to develop new services (Dhar & Stein, 2016). FinTech companies can reinterpret financial products of stakeholders by using this data to create more valuable offerings. They continuously refine and reinterpret stakeholder products as the external data-to-product-to-data cycle evolves. By integrating external data, FinTech companies drive innovation and increase the value and relevance of their services.

Stakeholders

FinTech companies can collaborate with multiple stakeholders to reinterpret and refine their products using a variety of data sources:

- Banks and financial institutions offer partnership opportunities to enhance a variety of financial products, including accounts, cards, payment solutions, loans, investments, and insurance.
- Government agencies, as a major source of financial data, provide valuable data sets that include information on taxation, social security, invoicing, payment systems, and production and consumption. FinTech companies can use this information to create innovative financial solutions.
- Private sector companies in commerce, retail, transportation, education, healthcare, manufacturing, tourism, and other sectors can collaborate with FinTech companies to share data and services, thereby facilitating the development of innovative financial products.

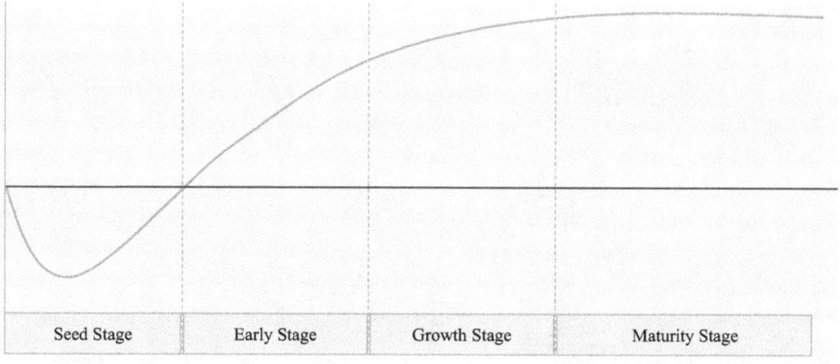

Fig. 1.3 Stages of FinTech lifecycle

1.3 FinTech Lifecycle

Figure 1.3 depicts the S-curve shape of the FinTech lifecycle, the seed, early, growth, and maturity stages.

The FinTech lifecycle consists of four stages, each of which presents unique challenges that must be overcome. Unlike traditional financial theory, which follows a linear lifecycle with predefined funding sources, FinTech sector is considerably more complex and dynamic (Bonini & Capizzi, 2019). Although the FinTech lifecycle often begins with an innovative, digital-first concept, long-term success depends on regulatory compliance, effective governance, and a robust growth strategy (Grant Thornton, 2019). In order to survive, FinTech companies must continuously innovate and challenge conventional financial models.

1.3.1 Seed Stage

The seed stage is divided into three periods: pre-seed, seed, and late seed. During this stage, FinTech companies are not yet fully institutionalized or corporatized. Instead, they focus on refining their business models and achieving key milestones to build a solid foundation for future growth.

Figure 1.4 shows the inner periods of the seed stage and the deepest level of the FinTech lifecycle.

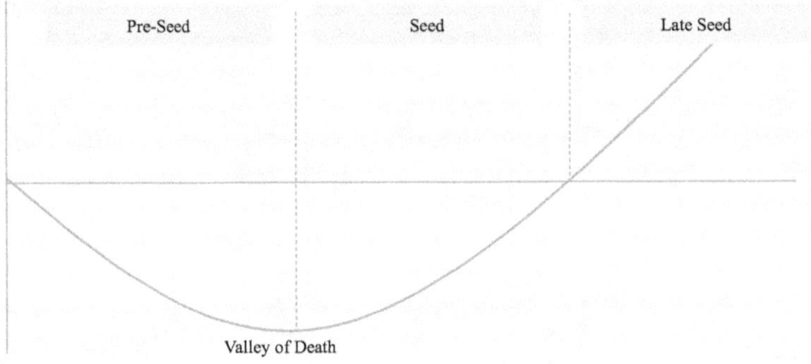

Fig. 1.4 Seed stage

Pre-Seed Period

The pre-seed period marks the beginning of the FinTech lifecycle when a simple idea is transformed into a compelling business concept. This period is particularly risky because the product has not yet been developed or launched. As the earliest and most precarious stage of FinTech funding, it involves conducting market research, creating a business plan and product prototype, and assembling a capable team (Arnold et al., 2024). During this time, access to venture capital is critical to the establishment of a FinTech company (Haddad & Hornuf, 2019). FinTech companies typically operate on a limited budget and often rely on insider funding (Campanella et al., 2013). However, this limited funding can hinder research and development, making cost-effective and innovative solutions essential for success.

Choosing the right technology is critical, as it serves as the backbone of FinTech sector. Entrepreneurs should seek guidance from experts, consultants, angel investors, and other stakeholders to refine their technology options. Thorough evaluation and pre-testing are essential to ensure that the selected technology meets budget constraints. Technology transfer and partnerships can further reduce development costs. Assembling the right team is a critical factor during the pre-seed period. Diverse team with complementary skill sets significantly increases the chances of success for FinTech ventures (CB Insights, 2019). Strong team is also the first step toward institutionalization. In addition, early regulatory compliance is critical. FinTech companies need to apply for licenses and permits from the outset to ensure smoother operations in later stages. Addressing regulatory requirements early on helps mitigate legal risks and facilitates scalability.

Seed Period

The seed period begins when a FinTech company establishes its corporate identity. During this time, the company develops a prototype proof of concept (Brown, 2021) while refining its business models, marketing strategies, and financial projections. Entrepreneurs should prioritize four core strategies: funding, marketing, growth, and technology, as each is essential to success during the seed period.

- Funding strategy focuses on securing financial support from both internal sources and external investors. Key components include assessing capital needs, diversifying funding options, managing investor relations, clearly articulating the value proposition, balancing risk, and reward, conducting pre-valuation assessments, and preparing business models, financial projections, and long-term goals.
- Marketing strategy involves identifying target users and planning outreach efforts. It includes market and competitive analysis, user profiling, product diversification, value proposition development, product launch planning, distribution channel selection, pricing strategy, and data-driven optimization.
- Growth strategies require identifying opportunities for scaling and executing expansion plans. This process includes developing investment strategies, forming partnerships, embracing digital innovation, implementing user acquisition and retention strategies, optimizing workflows, improving efficiencies, and establishing sustainable revenue models.
- Technology strategy outlines how technology aligns with business objectives and maintains competitiveness. It includes digitization processes, technology frameworks, user interface design, security, digital privacy, trend analysis, leveraging AI, and ensuring scalability and performance improvements.

Valley of Death

Every FinTech company encounters a critical phase known as the "valley of death," often considered the most perilous phase in its lifecycle. This phase occurs between the startup and commercialization stages and is characterized by limited structure, resources, and expertise (Markham, 2002). During this phase, FinTech companies struggle to generate sufficient cash flow to cover expenses and sustain operations, often facing the deepest cash deficits of their lifecycle. The primary challenge is not just significant financial losses, but rather an overwhelming cash shortfall that threatens survival. While capital injections and borrowing can provide temporary relief, it is critical to address cash flow issues promptly to ensure long-term viability.

To survive the valley of death, FinTech companies must take strategic steps to ensure financial stability and long-term growth. Effective cash management is critical. Entrepreneurs should analyze financial data to anticipate cash shortfalls and implement preventative measures to maintain liquidity. Equally important is optimizing spending, which involves reducing non-essential expenses, deferring non-urgent investments, and identifying cost-saving opportunities. Exploring alternative funding sources can provide critical financial support. Options include angel investors, venture capital, and direct loans, which can help companies bridge the gap between startup and commercialization. Accelerating growth is also critical. Completing product development, increasing revenue through sales, expanding user base, and implementing targeted marketing strategies can help build momentum and financial stability.

FinTech companies can successfully navigate this challenging phase and move toward sustainable success by effectively managing resources, securing strategic funding, and driving growth. Reevaluating the revenue model, exploring new revenue streams and assessing product differentiation are essential to achieving financial stability. Entrepreneurs must remain agile in their decision-making and adapt to changing circumstances while maintaining transparent communication with investors. Learning from mistakes, such as budgeting and planning errors, fosters continuous improvement. Understanding user expectations and redesigning products to improve cash flow are critical to long-term success. Ignoring user feedback is a well-documented path to failure, and ignoring user input is one of the most fatal mistakes for FinTech companies (CB Insights, 2019). Integrating user feedback is essential, as establishing dynamic communication channels and analyzing workflows leads to better product refinement. Entrepreneurs should regularly evaluate their teams to identify new skills and talents that can provide a competitive advantage. If a FinTech product fails, it is often wiser to withdraw it from the market than to rush to address the challenges. In addition, entrepreneurs should avoid becoming overly attached to their FinTech ideas and products.

Market Entry

This phase marks the launch of FinTech products (Weinmayr et al., 2020). During this phase, FinTech companies must define their target market, analyze user profiles, personalize their offerings, develop competitive pricing strategies, and create intuitive user interfaces. By successfully implementing these strategies, FinTech companies can gain a competitive advantage by delivering products that meet user expectations and increase engagement. Rapid go-to-market programs and targeted advertising campaigns effectively introduce the product and brand to user base during this phase. Well-planned campaigns enhance marketing efforts, increase visibility, and accelerate user acquisition. FinTech companies can gather valuable user feedback, refine their offerings, and potentially generate early revenue through mockups, prototypes, or beta versions. In addition, leveraging digital channels expands access to potential users, strengthens market positioning, and provides a competitive edge.

Commercialization

The commercialization phase is a strategic approach to product launch, pricing, marketing, and distribution. FinTech companies commercialize their products through technological and financial innovation (Brandl & Hornuf, 2020). Setting competitive prices is essential to ensure alignment with the product's perceived value, cost structure, and users' willingness to pay. Marketing efforts are critical to attract potential users by highlighting key features, benefits, and overall value proposition. This phase also includes strategic sales initiatives, product management, market research, promotional campaigns, advertising, and the selection of optimal distribution channels. Well-structured go-to-market strategy increases visibility, strengthens market positioning, and accelerates user adoption.

Late Seed Period

Late seed period bridges the seed and early stages of the FinTech lifecycle. During this time, successful product launches, initial user acquisition, accelerated commercialization efforts, and clear growth potential are significant milestones. However, most FinTech companies still require additional funding to reach full operational capacity and expand into new markets. The focus shifts to securing further investment, emphasizing refinement, and demonstrating business progress. From an investor perspective, the sales cycle during this period is critical in assessing the viability and scalability of the business (Weinmayr et al., 2020). Funds raised during this period are used to enhance existing products, accelerate marketing efforts, acquire new users, and optimize operations, business models, and expansion strategies. This period also marks the beginning of institutionalization, during which FinTech companies address structural weaknesses, improve organizational efficiency, and prepare for scaling.

1.3.2 *Early Stage*

The early stage of FinTech lifecycle is divided into two key periods: Series A and Series B. During this stage, a FinTech company's valuation is established and can fluctuate significantly, influenced by its ability to achieve or fail to meet critical milestones (Mercer Capital, 2018).

Figure 1.5 illustrates the ramp-up phase of the FinTech lifecycle, which includes the Series A and Series B periods.

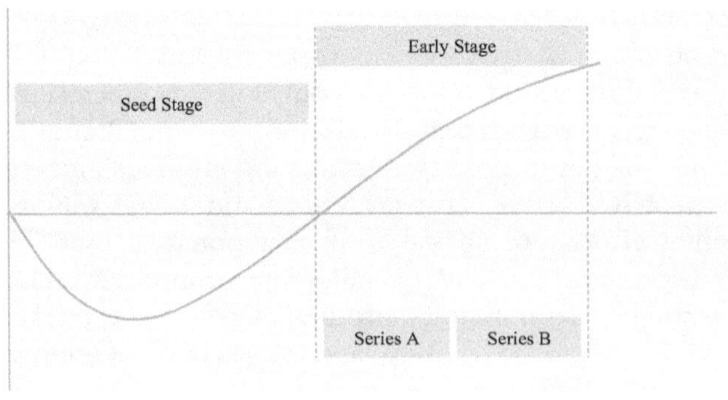

Fig. 1.5 Early stage

Series A

Series A is the first major round of funding and marks a crucial period in the growth and investment trajectory of FinTech companies (Schueffel, 2017). FinTech companies have a competitive advantage in attracting investor interest due to their scalability potential. Depending on the success of previous funding rounds, investors-including venture capital firms, angel investors, and private equity firms-prioritize long-term viability when evaluating Series A opportunities. During this period, it is essential to demonstrate recurring revenue (Weinmayr et al., 2020). Factors such as market size, growth potential, competitive landscape, financial performance, and management strength significantly influence early valuations. Successfully securing Series A funding lays the foundation for further expansion and product development.

Series B

Series B is the second major funding round for FinTech growth, attracting a diverse group of investors, including private equity firms (Schueffel, 2017). This period builds on the momentum of previous funding rounds and signifies continued expansion. During this period, scalability becomes a primary focus, with user acquisition, technology infrastructure, and market expansion as key priorities. FinTech companies focus on developing new products, increasing market share, and scaling operations. Engineering and marketing teams experience exponential growth during this time, and top management structures are solidified. Series B funding typically involves larger investments and attracts institutional investors such as specialized venture capital firms, large mutual funds, and private equity firms. FinTech companies in this period are expected to achieve higher valuations, reflecting their growth trajectory and market potential.

1.3.3 Growth Stage

This stage consists of two key periods: Series C and Series C + +. During this growth stage, FinTech companies have validated the basic assumptions of their business models but have not yet fully scaled to reach their maximum potential (Murthy & Faz, 2021).

Figure 1.6 shows the growth stage of FinTech, highlighting the Series C and Series C+ + rounds.

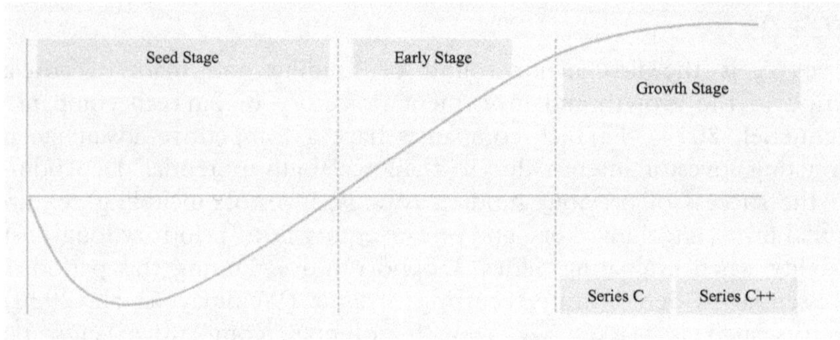

Fig. 1.6 Growth stage

Series C

Series C is the third major funding round aimed at scaling FinTech growth and attracting investments from hedge funds, investment banks, and other institutional investors (Schueffel, 2017). During this period, FinTech companies seek large capital injections to support expansion while maintaining profitability. This period is characterized by increased competition, with investors focusing on valuation, sustainable growth, and market positioning. In addition, Series C funding often is a precursor to an IPO, as going public provides access to a broader investor base. To align with IPO goals, FinTech companies must refine their strategies, optimize operations, and ensure that their financial performance meets market expectations.

Series C + + (Series D, Series E, Series F, Series G, Series H…)

Series C + + refers to extended funding rounds that occur when a FinTech company is uncertain about securing the expected funding during its Series C round. These rounds involve the issuing of additional shares to investors (KPMG, 2024) and are designed to sustain growth and extend the financial runway. This phase is characterized by internationalization, with a focus on increasing market share, developing new products, and entering global markets. Maintaining a high company valuation and preparing for an IPO remain top priorities to ensure competitiveness. The interpretation of Series C + + can vary. From a pessimistic perspective, it may indicate challenges in achieving growth targets or declining investor confidence. Conversely, an optimistic view suggests that the FinTech company is postponing its IPO due to regulatory requirements, accounting compliance, economic uncertainties, or market volatility. The company may be prioritizing building long-term relationships with qualified investors rather than going public.

1.3.4 Maturity Stage

FinTech has become a major market player in the maturity stage. FinTech companies prioritize sustainability and measurable positive outcomes for users (Murthy & Faz, 2021). They may also be preparing for a potential exit strategy, either through acquisition or an IPO (Arnold et al., 2024).

Figure 1.7 illustrates the maturity stage of the FinTech lifecycle as it navigates the money and capital markets.

Initial Public Offering

Going public is an irreversible decision in the journey of FinTech companies seeking access to capital markets. However, conducting an IPO requires extensive financial and operational processes to meet the strict requirements of public markets (Deloitte, 2021). During this period, the company offers its shares to the public, which requires full compliance with capital market regulations, generally accepted accounting principles, and international financial reporting standards. FinTech companies go to the public for several reasons. First, stock exchanges facilitate fair price discovery, with share prices determined by the dynamics of supply and

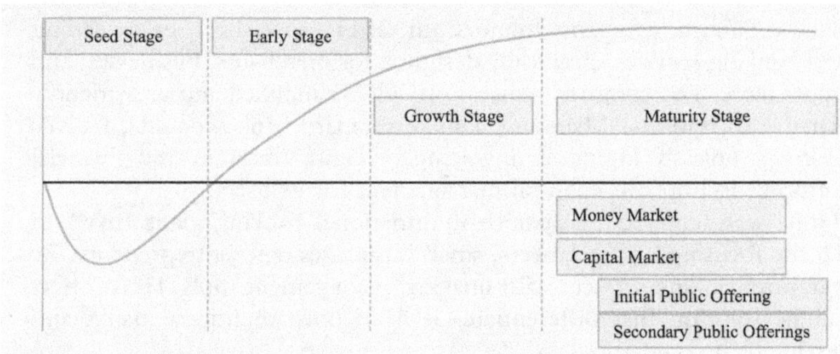

Fig. 1.7 Maturity stage

demand. Because FinTech companies often operate in specific market niches, an accurate assessment of their performance in these segments is critical to valuation (Mercer Capital, 2018). Second, an IPO increases a FinTech company's credibility with banks and financial institutions, resulting in more favorable credit terms. However, the primary motivation for an IPO is to raise capital for growth. The funds raised can also strengthen equity, reduce debt, and improve the debt-to-equity ratio, thereby enhancing financial stability and long-term growth potential.

IPO can further institutionalize FinTech, increasing its market penetration and financial stability. Effective cash flow management and share sales ensure liquidity, while access to a broader investor base creates new funding opportunities. An increase in paid in capital increases valuation and market capitalization, strengthening competitive positioning. An IPO also provides a strategic exit for early investors and enhances the company's reputation. This increased credibility fosters greater trust among investors, partners, users, vendors, and employees. In addition, a publicly traded FinTech company is more likely to attract top talent, which improves job satisfaction and overall quality of the workforce. From a financial perspective, an IPO allows a company to raise more capital per share or issue fewer shares for a given amount of funding. For investors, it diversifies portfolios, reduces concentration risk, and stabilizes market capitalization. Finally, an IPO establishes a mark-to-market valuation that is essential for future fundraisings, secondary offerings, mergers, and acquisitions.

Case Study 1.1: Holvi

Holvi, a Finnish company founded in 2011, specializes in providing digital banking services specifically designed for merchants, businesses, and entrepreneurs. The company aims to provide a simplified and user-friendly alternative to traditional banking. Unlike standard bank accounts, Holvi's platform seamlessly integrates invoicing, expense tracking, and financial monitoring to improve financial management for its users.

Holvi was acquired by Spanish multinational banking giant BBVA in 2016, by focusing on freelancers, small businesses, and entrepreneurs. By integrating banking services with financial management tools, Holvi offers a unique solution that differentiates it from both traditional banks and other FinTech competitors.

Holvi's Key Products (Holvi, 2024)

- Business Debit Cards
- Business Credit Cards
- Virtual Cards
- Billing and E-Invoicing
- Payment-to-Invoice Reconciliation
- Bookkeeping Preparation
- Export Reports for Tax Filing
- Accounting Integrations
- ATM Instant Top-Ups

With the increasing demand for flexible and modern financial solutions, Holvi is strategically positioned to expand its presence in the digital banking sector. The company is expected to enter new markets and develop innovative products that meet the evolving needs of its users. By consistently adapting to market trends, Holvi will strengthen its status as a leading provider of digital banking services for entrepreneurs, professionals, and small businesses.

CHAPTER 2

Business Model

Abstract This chapter examines the creation of FinTech, focusing on business models, strategic partnerships, and value propositions. It highlights the impact of digital technologies, personalized services, and financial inclusion on user satisfaction. The success of FinTech operations depends on effective cost management, competitive pricing, and continuous product innovation. The chapter explores various revenue models, including subscription, pay-per-use, freemium, and free trial options, as well as pricing strategies such as value-based, competitive, and cost-based approaches. Furthermore, it evaluates pricing models, including fixed, variable, mixed, and tiered structures, and analyzes their roles in stabilizing profitability while enhancing user acquisition and retention.

Keywords Business model · Revenue models · Pricing

A business model is a set of decisions designed to maximize the economic value of FinTech. It outlines how an organization creates, delivers, and captures value (Schueffel, 2017). The impact of FinTech companies on the evolution of the financial sector is largely dependent on their business models (Koroleva, 2022). This model includes key objectives, strategies, and operations required for success. To remain competitive,

T. Geçer and V. Akgiray, *The Financial Technology Revolution*,
https://doi.org/10.1007/978-3-031-92048-6_2

FinTech companies need to develop models that prioritize digital innovation over conventional methods, leveraging their unique strengths and technological advantages.

2.1 Components of Business Model

Osterwalder and Pigneur (2005) define a business model as a framework consisting of nine key dimensions: customer segments, value propositions, channels, customer relationships, key resources, key activities, key partnerships, revenue streams, and cost structure (Alt & Huch, 2022).

2.1.1 Key Partnerships

Key partnerships are a critical element of the FinTech business model. These collaborations focus on working with financial institutions and technology companies. They fall into three primary categories, each offering unique opportunities for growth and innovation.

Technology Partnership

Technology partnerships facilitate the development, implementation, and enhancement of secure technology infrastructures. These collaborations provide to perform IT systems, manage databases, and ensure robust security measures. By partnering with third-party experts, FinTech companies can adopt innovative technologies, refine products, scale operations, and expand into global markets.

Strategic Partnership

By forming strategic partnerships, FinTech companies aim for long-term sustainability. Partnering with other companies can enhance marketing and sales strategies, increase revenue, and expand user base. These partnerships can also reduce user acquisition costs and create opportunities to explore new markets. In addition, outsourcing specialized tasks to third-parties can significantly improve FinTech operations.

Investment Partnership

Sustainable funding is critical for FinTech companies to achieve their goals and meet their capital needs. Investment partners provide the necessary resources for product development, marketing, and technology infrastructure. Beyond financial support, they provide strategic insight that drives growth and improves operational efficiency. Their extensive networks create opportunities, strengthen competitive advantages, and increase user confidence.

2.1.2 *Key Activities*

Key activities are the essential functions and processes that deliver value to users and sustain FinTech operations (Imenso Software, 2025). Sound business strategy should align policies and practices with both short-term and long-term goals. Well-structured strategies are critical for sustainable growth and maintaining competitive advantage. Core components include strategic planning, financial management, operations, marketing, and human resource development.

- Strategic management involves setting future goals, creating a robust business model, and developing growth strategies while ensuring the efficient allocation of resources.
- Financial management improves economic performance by balancing revenues and expenses, effectively budgeting, monitoring cash flow, and ensuring accurate financial reporting.
- Operations management focuses on optimizing processes to improve efficiency and productivity.
- Marketing management involves identifying target markets, developing strategies, promoting products, and improving user acquisition and retention.
- Human resource management implements policies to attract top talent, promote professional development, and monitor performance and career planning.

2.1.3 *Key Resources*

Key resources allow FinTech companies to effectively utilize technology, capital, and human resources to ensure smooth business operations (Ankenbrand et al., 2016).

Technology Resources

Effective technology management is critical to streamlining processes and maintaining a competitive edge. The right technology streamlines workflows, improves interactions, and delivers a seamless experience. Flexible and scalable framework enables rapid adaptation to market changes, strengthening the market position of FinTech companies.

Human Resources

FinTech companies are essentially high-tech businesses, so human capital is critical to their success. They require highly skilled talent to drive innovation and maintain competitiveness (Koroleva, 2022). It is critical to assemble an excellent team with complementary expertise, while ensuring an optimal team size to achieve labor cost efficiency. Rather than prioritizing headcount growth, FinTech companies should focus on workforce optimization and operational efficiency to maximize productivity and ensure long-term sustainability.

Financial Resources

Effective financial management enables FinTech companies to sustain operations and drive growth. Strategic resource allocation ensures that these companies can meet business needs while capitalizing on new opportunities. Appropriate financial oversight promotes stability by managing cash flow and addressing payment challenges, thereby supporting key initiatives such as product development, marketing, and expansion. Robust financial resource base increases resilience during economic uncertainties, while selecting appropriate funding sources minimizes financial costs and optimizes capital acquisition. Well-defined financing strategy builds investor confidence, enhances competitiveness, and fosters trust among users and stakeholders.

2.1.4 *Value Proposition*

Value propositions outline the products and services offered by FinTech companies and the unique value they create for users (Ankenbrand et al., 2016). As the foundation of FinTech's business model, these propositions provide a competitive advantage and enhance user experience. Strong, user-centric value proposition is essential to achieving success and converting short-term satisfaction into long-term loyalty. To attract and retain users, FinTech companies must clearly articulate the benefits and features of their offerings to ensure that their value proposition remains compelling and aligned with market needs.

Ease of Use

Ease of use is critical for FinTech products, allowing users to complete transactions quickly and effortlessly. Well-designed, intuitive interface with streamlined workflows greatly improves overall user experience. FinTech companies should prioritize clarity and simplicity in navigation, avoiding overly complex designs that may hinder accessibility. Fast and efficient transaction processing is essential to meet user expectations.

Speed

FinTech companies must balance speed and security to deliver a seamless user experience. Instant transaction processing, quick verification, and prompt responses to user requests are essential to maintaining efficiency. Real-time access to data, accounts, and transaction menus further enhances user expectations and ensures smooth, uninterrupted service.

Personalization

Personalization is critical for FinTech companies looking to increase user satisfaction. By leveraging AI, ML, and DL, FinTech companies can customize their products and gain deeper business intelligence insights into user behavior, preferences, and habits. Smooth communication channels facilitate smooth interactions, while tailored services cultivate a sense of value and trust, ultimately strengthening user engagement and loyalty.

Accessibility

FinTech accessibility requires the availability of products at all times and from any location across various platforms, ensuring consistent functionality. FinTech companies must provide intuitive mobile applications and responsive web platforms that deliver seamless services. Around-the-clock support are essential for addressing user concerns, while strict compliance with global security standards protects digital privacy. Regularly integrating feedbacks improves accessibility, and maintaining high uptime ensures reliable service delivery.

Innovation

Innovation reshapes the future of FinTech and can be categorized into four key groups.

- Innovation in Product: Product innovation focuses on identifying user needs and creating forward-thinking financial solutions. It is driven by user feedback, market trends, and emerging technologies to ensure continuous development and relevance. Successful FinTech companies must prioritize innovation in both product development and operations (Lee & Teo, 2015).
- Innovation in Process: This innovation enhances usability by creating smooth interfaces, responsive mobile applications, and automated processes. By prioritizing intuitive design, they can improve accessibility and increase user engagement.
- Innovation in Security: This innovation aims to protect sensitive data, maintain digital privacy, and ensure compliance with global security standards. Advanced security techniques and fraud prevention measures build trust and reliability.
- Innovation in Technology: Technology innovation leverages the latest advances to streamline processes, customize services, and create next-generation products.

Pricing

FinTech companies typically use two main pricing strategies to attract and grow their user base: offer a superior product at a higher price or offer a basic product at a lower price. Some FinTech companies adopt aggressive pricing strategies to gain market share (ECB, 2018), ensuring a competitive advantage and facilitating rapid market entry. Pricing decisions are influenced by financial needs and market conditions (Neubert, 2017). To optimize pricing and minimize operating costs, FinTech companies should reduce on-premises investments by leveraging outsourcing, licensing, and leasing options. Prioritizing high-value services and maximizing return on investment are critical to long-term profitability. Efficiency measures, such as reducing both fixed and variable costs, help lower total cost per product and maintain price competitiveness.

2.1.5 *Key Revenue Streams*

FinTech companies must develop a profitable revenue model that is consistent with a competitive pricing strategy. Revenue model outlines how a company will generate revenue through different revenue streams (Osterwalder et al., 2005), the products it offers, and its pricing strategy. The most common revenue streams include interest, commissions, transaction fees, licensing fees, advertising, and data monetization (Ankenbrand et al., 2016). Additional revenue streams may include hardware and software sales, currency exchange gains, up-selling, cross-selling, API monetization, insight reporting, and consulting services.

Successful FinTech companies often operate with low profit margins, prioritizing user acquisition to achieve profitability through high transaction volumes (Lee & Teo, 2015). Therefore, FinTech companies need to keep their marginal costs below zero.

2.1.6 *Cost Structure*

Cost structure refers to the financial implications of resource allocation in a business model (Osterwalder et al., 2005). While cost structures can vary, a balance between revenues and expenses is essential for long-term sustainability. Major expenses typically include personnel, marketing, finance, technology, and consulting costs.

Personnel costs can be substantial in the early stages, depending on the size and composition of the team. Marketing expenses are also significant and include user acquisition, product promotion, and branding efforts. Effective financial management is critical to balance equity and debt financing to support continued growth. In addition, technology costs—including software, hardware, and networking—are critical for scalability, efficiency, and speed. Consulting fees may also be required for services such as technology integration, accounting, tax, and regulatory compliance.

2.1.7 *Distribution Channels*

Distribution channels determine how these companies deliver services and engage with users (Osterwalder et al., 2005). While most companies rely primarily on digital platforms, many employ multichannel strategies to expand their reach (Gimpel et al., 2018). Identifying the most effective distribution channels improves user acquisition and market penetration. Tailoring products to each channel increases effectiveness; for example, a mobile application is ideal for an app-based platform, while a payment solution is more appropriate for an e-commerce website.

2.1.8 *User Segmentation*

Successful business development begins with effective user segmentation. The basic assumption is that users have unique characteristics but share common needs (Smeureanu et al., 2013). User segmentation allows FinTech companies to identify target users, tailor products, and improve marketing strategies. Process involves grouping users based on demographics, financial capacities, behaviors, expectations, and preferences. Data analysis creates detailed user profiles that distinguish segments such as young adults, women, students, and professionals while highlighting their unique characteristics. Segmentation also assesses the size and growth potential of each group, facilitating the design of hyper-personalized products and targeted marketing campaigns. Ongoing monitoring and analysis is essential to refine strategies, identify successes, and address areas for improvement.

2.2 Categories of Users

FinTech companies can categorize users into five separate groups: non-banked, unbanked, underbanked, banked, and overbanked.

2.2.1 Non-Banked

This category includes individuals who do not have legal access to banking and financial services, such as infants, children, and individuals with certain disabilities or legal incapacities.

2.2.2 Unbanked

The unbanked population lacks access to formal financial services due to limited availability, reliance on cash, and distrust of the banking system (Holt & Littlewood, 2014; Schueffel, 2017). This group may include marginalized communities, people with disabilities, students, youth, immigrants, and people with language barriers. Many individuals seek alternative financial services, such as payday loans and check cashing, due to low income, low assets, and limited access to credit. To promote financial inclusion, regulators, banks, and FinTech companies must develop technology-based solutions (Pramani & Iyer, 2023). Mobile-based financial solutions can increase access to credit and reduce inefficiencies for individuals (UN, 2023). FinTech companies can bridge the gap by providing accessible financial solutions, simplified tools, and financial literacy programs. Intuitive mobile applications, personalized guidance, and partnerships with universities and nonprofits are essential to overcome barriers such as low digital literacy and mistrust.

Figure 2.1 illustrates users in banking industry based on their level of engagement with banking services.

2.2.3 Underbanked

The underbanked have limited access to formal financial services and often rely on cash and alternative solutions instead of traditional banking products such as credit cards or loans (Holt & Littlewood, 2014; Schueffel, 2017). While they use bank services for basic transactions, they typically prefer non-traditional credit options due to mistrust of banks and financial constraints. Cash remains essential to their economic participation,

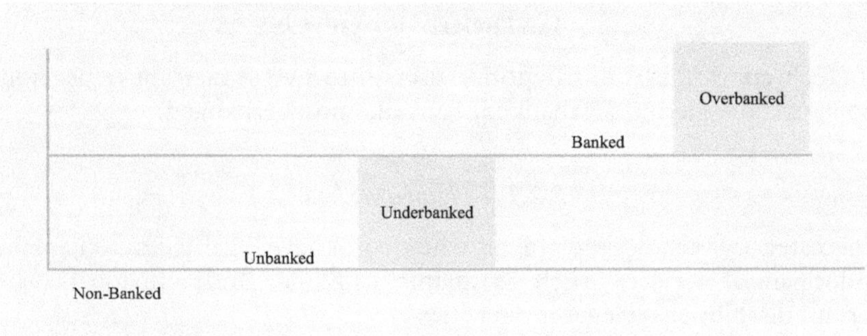

Fig. 2.1 Categories of Users

making it critical for banks to ensure continued access (WSBI, 2021). This group faces barriers such as migration status, age, disability, education level, and rural residence, all of which contribute to financial and digital illiteracy. It is important to recognize that underbanked represent a distinct demographic with unique challenges that require tailored policy interventions (Barcellos & Zamarro, 2019). FinTech companies should conduct market research to better understand their needs and encourage adoption through discounted or free financial products to promote financial inclusion. Simplifying transactions, reducing platform complexity, and implementing alternative scoring methods can increase accessibility. In addition, offering easy-to-use digital products with mobile access while ensuring compliance with security, privacy, and regulatory standards can encourage long-term engagement.

2.2.4 Banked

The banked category includes individuals and businesses that use banking services to manage their finances. While they primarily rely on traditional banks, FinTech companies can attract this demographic by offering innovative solutions that enhance existing services. Banked users perform routine transactions efficiently and are highly engaged with mobile applications and web platforms. They trust digital technologies, frequently use digital wallets, and prefer electronic payments. They also have convenient access to financial services such as loans and credit cards that help them manage their assets and meet their financial obligations.

2.2.5 *Overbanked*

The overbanked are individuals and businesses that have multiple banking relationships, use multiple financial products, and carry significant debt. They often rely on credit, payment cards, and multiple banking services, often switching between institutions to secure better rates and benefits. Their loyalty to a single institution is typically low, and managing multiple accounts can complicate their financial health. Although they are generally tech-savvy, they often struggle with budgeting, account tracking, and debt management, which can lead to challenges such as over-borrowing, poor credit scores, and complex debt obligations. It is important to recognize that underbanked and overbanked represent distinct groups, each with unique circumstances that may require different policy interventions (Barcellos & Zamarro, 2019).

Financial institutions should offer personalized tools to increase user engagement and retention, including budgeting applications, spending controls, and tailored financial advice. Value-added products such as insurance, investment options, and loyalty programs can significantly improve user experience. Open banking-enabled account aggregation simplifies financial oversight, while debt management strategies such as refinancing, programmable payments, and consolidation-help reduce financial stress. Robo-advisory services for deposits, loans and investments can facilitate informed decision-making. Educating users about credit scores and responsible borrowing practices is essential to rebuilding trust. Working with wealth management firms to develop structured repayment plans and negotiate better terms can strengthen long-term relationships.

2.3 Revenue Models

Revenue models are complex and shaped by a variety of factors, including trust, value, perception, timing, and relevance (Oliver Wyman, 2018). As a result, FinTech companies must develop revenue streams early in their operations and continually refine their models as they evolve.

Figure 2.2 illustrates the primary revenue streams in FinTech, which include subscription and pay-per-use models, as well as freemium and free trial marketing strategies.

Fig. 2.2 Revenue Models

2.3.1 Subscription Model

The subscription model charges users a fixed, recurring fee for access to content, products, or services, regardless of usage (Deloitte, 2023; Lindström et al., 2023). In FinTech sector, users subscribe based on features, pricing, and user experience, paying upfront for a planned service. To be successful, FinTech companies must clearly communicate the benefits of their products, justify recurring fees, and offer flexible plans tailored to users' needs. Transparent fee disclosure is essential, and pricing should reflect value, market trends, and competitive dynamics. This approach relies on ongoing engagement, regular product updates, and the cultivation of strong customer relationships (Lindström et al., 2023). Personalized communications, seamless support, and hassle-free cancelation processes build trust and encourage user reactivation.

2.3.2 Pay-Per-Use Model

The pay-per-use model charges users based on actual usage, such as per minute or per transaction, providing flexibility and cost efficiency (Deloitte, 2023). Users only pay for what they use, making it budget-friendly and eliminating unnecessary expenses. For FinTech companies, this model ensures sustainable revenue, improves financial stability, and supports scalable growth as user base expands. Aligning cost with perceived value improves user satisfaction and drives adoption. However, pricing strategies can influence user behavior and limit usage (Arani et al., 2023). Challenges include revenue volatility, uncertainty about product value, and billing complexity. FinTech companies must implement efficient billing systems, maintain transparent pricing, and provide real-time usage tracking to ensure stability, build trust, mitigate risk, and enhance user experience.

2.3.3 Freemium Model

The freemium model combines free and premium services, providing basic functionality for free while encouraging users to upgrade to paid versions (EC, 2015). This acquisition strategy encourages user adoption through limited free access (Deloitte, 2023). Access to content, storage, or usage is restricted to incentivize users to upgrade (Hamari et al., 2020). Unlike traditional pricing models, the freemium approach functions as a marketing strategy that converts non-paying users by demonstrating the value of the service. The free version provides basic functionality, while premium tiers offer advanced features. By effectively balancing free offerings with compelling premium features, FinTech companies can improve user engagement, increase conversion rates, and drive long-term growth.

Freemium Types

- Capacity-Based Freemium: This freemium model provides free access up to a certain limit, after which users must pay for additional capacity. This strategy encourages upgrades by allowing users to experience the value of the service before committing to a premium version.
- Time-Based Freemium: This model provides free access for a limited period of time before payment is required (Pujol, 2010). Users can evaluate the product before deciding whether to upgrade or discontinue their use.
- Feature-Based Freemium: This model provides a basic version for free while charging for advanced features (Anderson, 2009). Users can access basic features for free, while premium features are only available behind a paywall. The free version must be appealing enough to attract users, and the premium features should provide significant value to encourage conversions.

Prerequisites for the Freemium Model

For the freemium model to be successful, there must be a clear connection between the free and premium services that encourages users to upgrade. The free version should offer enough capacity, time, and features to attract users while subtly motivating them to upgrade to the premium versions.

Because marginal costs per user are minimal (EC, 2015), a successful freemium model minimizes service costs by leveraging automated, hyper-personalized customer relationships (Holm & Günzel-Jensen, 2017). Although there are costs associated with non-paying users, FinTech companies must balance user acquisition and conversion rates to maintain profitability. The freemium model thrives on a large user base but may face challenges in smaller markets. Implementing tiered pricing for individuals and businesses can help maximize revenue. Even non-paying users add value by providing marketing insights and conversion opportunities. Understanding user behavior is a key competitive advantage for freemium businesses (Holm & Günzel-Jensen, 2017).

Advantages of the Freemium Model

The freemium model is a demand generation strategy (Pujol, 2010) that attracts users, increases conversion rates, and reduces acquisition and retention costs. Allowing users to experience the product first-hand demonstrates its value and encourages premium upgrades, driving revenue growth and market expansion (Hamari et al., 2020). Future research could examine user perceptions prior to adoption to gain a deeper understanding of conversion dynamics. Maintaining relationships with non-paying users fosters engagement and strengthens long-term connections. Large user base, comprising both free and premium users, enhances the competitiveness of FinTech companies and accelerates market entry. This model also facilitates up-selling and cross-selling, maximizing revenue potential. Additionally, it enables the aggregation of valuable data on user behavior, preferences, and habits, which can be used to refine marketing strategies and product offerings. By leveraging these business intelligence insights, FinTech companies can improve user targeting, enhance user experience, and sustain long-term growth.

Disadvantages of the Freemium Model

While the freemium model offers several advantages, it also presents significant challenges. Non-paying users may be reluctant to upgrade if the free version adequately meets their needs, which can diminish the perceived value of premium offerings. To address this issue, FinTech companies must develop targeted marketing strategies that highlight the unique benefits of the premium version and effectively communicate its value. There are significant development, infrastructure, and advertising costs associated with maintaining a free product. As the non-paying user base grows, these costs can erode profitability and accelerate cash burn, especially if the ratio of paying to non-paying users becomes unsustainable. Low conversion rates may indicate that the free version is too comprehensive or that premium features lack appeal. In such cases, FinTech companies should re-evaluate their pricing models, marketing strategies, and premium offerings.

Improving customer support and engagement for non-paying users is essential to maintain satisfaction and protect brand reputation. In addition, offering a free product in a market where competitors charge for it can create a competitive disadvantage. Effectively managing free and premium pricing structures requires clear differentiation, which can be challenging as it involves trade-offs between user base growth and revenue generation (Pujol, 2010). If the value of premium upgrades is not effectively communicated, users may continue to use the free version, requiring tailored marketing strategies for different user segments.

2.3.4 Free Trial Model

The free trial model effectively attracts users and encourages premium upgrades by offering full access to features for a limited time (Chen, 2023). This approach allows users to evaluate the product's value before committing to a paid version or discontinuing use. By providing hands-on experience, free trials enhance conversion rates and generate short-term revenue. FinTech companies must consider competitive factors when designing free trials, including their effectiveness, optimal duration, and post-trial pricing (Chen, 2023). Free trial fosters trust increases engagement, and strengthens long-term relationships, ultimately improving user adoption and retention.

Freemium vs. Free Trial

The freemium and free trial models are different marketing strategies. The freemium model offers a basic version of a product for free, encouraging incremental upgrades and fostering long-term engagement. In contrast, free trials provide full access to the product for a limited time, encouraging upgrades at the end of the trial period. The freemium model targets a broader user base with limited functionality, while free trials focus on specific users who can thoroughly evaluate the product before making a commitment. The freemium model allows unlimited use of limited functionality, while free trials offer full functionality for a limited time. Both models aim to increase user retention and conversion; however, free trials serve as a short-term strategy to accelerate paid adoption, while the freemium model prioritizes long-term engagement.

2.3.5 Pricing

The commercial success of FinTech companies depends on the alignment of their business models with a well-structured pricing strategy. Pricing has a direct impact on market share, product perception, and quality signaling (Guerreiro et al., 2012). An effective pricing strategy integrated with marketing efforts must consider target users, product types, and tailored pricing tools (Petrovska et al., 2019). Setting the optimal price maximizes product value and ensures long-term profitability. For sustainable growth, FinTech companies should prioritize price discovery, select the optimal pricing model, define value metrics, and establish appropriate price levels (Wehrs & Parker, 2020). Effective pricing depends on several factors, including product features, price elasticity, demand, competition, market size, and economic conditions. Price transparency and a well-defined strategy that emphasizes product benefits are essential for success. Using a combination of pricing models can maximize return on investment. In the short term, pricing is a key determinant of profitability; in the long term, it ensures business sustainability (Aggarwal et al., 2022). Pricing remains a significant challenge for FinTech companies, requiring a careful balance between setting prices high enough to generate revenue and avoiding levels that may discourage adoption (CB Insights, 2019).

2.3.6 Pricing Strategies

<u>Value-Based Pricing</u>

Value-based pricing sets prices according to users' willingness to pay, emphasizing perceived value rather than cost-based factors (PwC, 2019). This approach aligns pricing with the value of the product to users (Hinterhuber, 2008). Pricing must remain flexible to adapt to market changes and evolving user expectations (Wehrs & Parker, 2020). To be effective, value-based pricing should be part of a broader marketing strategy with tools tailored to specific user segments (Petrovska et al., 2019). Unlike traditional models, value-based pricing rewards FinTech companies for delivering positive outcomes rather than linking prices to effort or time spent (Deloitte, 2021c). Aligning prices with perceived value can reduce price sensitivity, increase profitability, and strengthen user satisfaction, loyalty, and brand reputation (Oliver Wyman, 2018).

However, perceived value is subjective and varies by user, requiring investment in communication and targeted marketing. Negative brand image can reduce perceived value, even for high-quality products. In competitive markets, strong product differentiation is critical to justify value-based pricing (PwC, 2019). This pricing, while effective, can sometimes appear unfair, so clear communication is essential. Continually refining pricing strategies through market research, user engagement, and transparent value communication is critical for long-term success.

Competitive Pricing

Competitive pricing aligns product prices with market rates for similar offerings, enabling FinTech companies to attract users and remain competitive (Revenue Management Labs, 2024). This strategy assumes that users evaluate products based on both price and features, with competitive analysis playing a critical role in pricing decisions (Hinterhuber, 2008). By monitoring market trends and competitor pricing, FinTech companies can strategically position their products to maintain market share and attract users. Key benefit of competitive pricing is its flexibility, allowing for rapid price adjustments in response to market fluctuations (Revenue Management Labs, 2024). This approach benefits new entrants by simplifying pricing structures and accelerating market penetration. As competitors' prices stabilize, users tend to prioritize quality and value, encouraging innovation and product improvement. Pricing below competitors can increase market share, strengthen positioning, and diversify revenue streams, ultimately contributing to financial stability.

However, there are risks associated with competitive pricing. Price wars can erode margins, while aggressive pricing strategies can diminish perceived product quality and damage brand equity. In addition, this approach does not take into account volatile production costs, which can pose a challenge to long-term sustainability. An over-reliance on competitive pricing can limit product differentiation and overlook specific user needs. In FinTech sector, calculating unit costs can be complex, and unclear competitive pricing undermines the effectiveness of this strategy. FinTech companies must balance affordability, differentiation, innovation, and cost efficiency to succeed. Ensuring profitability while remaining competitive requires a comprehensive assessment of market dynamics, user expectations, and product offerings.

Cost-Based Pricing

Cost-based pricing sets product prices based on production costs, which include fixed, variable, and operating expenses, as well as an additional profit margin (known as cost-plus pricing) (Guerreiro et al., 2012). This method calculates unit costs and integrates a percentage of administrative, commercial, and financial expenses (Hinterhuber, 2008). It is most effective when both costs and user expectations remain stable, although perceived value is also taken into account. Cost-based pricing ensures profitability by covering costs, promoting financial stability, and simplifying pricing decisions. By aligning prices with unit costs, this approach increases predictability and transparency, which fosters user trust and loyalty, especially when costs are stable.

Cost-based pricing has several limitations. One major drawback is that it often overlooks perceived value by focusing solely on cost. This oversight can lead to underpricing and missed revenue opportunities. In addition, cost-based pricing is less effective in service industries where unit cost calculations are complex. It also struggles in competitive or dynamic markets because it cannot account for shifts in demand or user willingness to pay. While it can be effective in industries where competitors' pricing is stable, it can reduce competitiveness in declining or disrupted markets. To remain sustainable, FinTech companies must balance cost-based pricing with market-driven strategies. By integrating internal cost assessments with external market conditions, they can maximize profitability while maintaining user engagement and competitiveness.

2.3.7 Pricing Models

Fixed Pricing

Fixed pricing model sets a stable, predetermined price for a product or service based on user value, total costs, target margins, and market competition. This strategy provides predictable revenue, reduces price volatility, and simplifies financial forecasting. Users benefit from a clear understanding of upfront costs through transparent pricing with no hidden fees. In addition, fixed pricing increases price stability, reduces disputes, and eliminates the need for negotiation. For example, in payment processing, users typically pay a fixed percentage per transaction, regardless of card type or transaction size.

But fixed pricing model has its limitations. One major drawback is cost sensitivity, especially for users processing large transactions that can incur significant fees (Payfirma, 2016). Setting prices too high can drive users to seek out lower-cost competitors, while setting prices too low can jeopardize profitability. Another challenge is inflexibility; fixed prices do not adjust to market fluctuations or rising costs, which can strain margins. This model is vulnerable to marginal costs and requires careful planning to remain competitive and sustainable (Wu & Pavlou, 2019).

Variable Pricing

Variable pricing adjusts prices based on usage levels or features accessed, providing flexibility that aligns with user behavior and expectations. This model increases user satisfaction by correlating costs with usage, promotes fairness, and encourages long-term commitment. Users pay less when usage is low and more as usage increases, making this approach particularly attractive to cost-conscious users. In addition, variable pricing increases profitability during peak sales periods and enables FinTech companies to respond quickly to competitors' pricing strategies, ensuring they remain competitive. It also effectively adapts to market trends, as higher usage reduces unit and marginal costs, lowering operating expenses and driving revenue growth.

Although, variable pricing presents several challenges. Users can become frustrated if costs do not scale in proportion to their usage, leading to dissatisfaction and potential churn. The lack of fixed pricing complicates marketing efforts, price communication, and competitive comparisons, as users may have difficulty estimating their total costs. Effectively managing the complexity of pricing, revenue tracking, and cost structures requires constant monitoring and adjustment. To be successful, FinTech companies must clearly communicate their pricing structures and ensure that they are perceived as fair. If users perceive the model as unfair or overly complex, trust can erode, negatively impacting user retention.

Mixed Pricing

Mixed pricing combines fixed and variable pricing models, allowing FinTech companies to tailor their strategies based on user expectations and market conditions. This model balances the predictability of fixed pricing with the flexibility of variable pricing, taking into account factors such as competition, market trends, target demographics, and product features. It accommodates both heavy and occasional users, maximizing revenue from frequent users while offering affordable options to others, thereby broadening user base. This adaptive model builds trust and encourages long-term loyalty.

Nevertheless, mixed pricing presents several challenges. The pricing structure can become complex, requiring ongoing monitoring and tier management to remain competitive. In addition, fixed component can increase costs for infrequent users, potentially leading to dissatisfaction, and lower retention rates. To be successful, FinTech companies must balance cost management with value delivery and ensure that users clearly understand the benefits of the pricing levels. If fixed fees are perceived as unfair or unclear, user confidence can erode, leading to increased churn. Effective communication of the value proposition and regular evaluation of pricing levels are essential to maintaining user satisfaction and long-term success.

Tiered Pricing

Tiered pricing model categorizes prices into predefined levels, allowing users to choose a service that best meets their needs. Fees are bundled in each tier, meaning that individual transaction costs are not explicitly disclosed (Payfirma, 2016). Unlike fixed, variable, or mixed pricing, tiered pricing offers multiple options with different features, benefits, and usage limits. Costs increase as users progress to higher tiers, allowing FinTech companies to target different user segments by offering budget-friendly lower tiers and premium options for advanced features. Tiered pricing is often more effective than fixed pricing because it accommodates different needs and provides a tailored, cost-effective experience (Wu & Pavlou, 2019). By offering essential features at a lower cost in entry-level tiers and advanced features at premium prices in higher tiers, FinTech companies can attract a broader user base. This flexibility allows pricing strategies to adapt to changes in the market, increasing user retention and profitability.

In addition, tiered pricing improves user satisfaction by providing value at multiple price levels, fostering long-term loyalty.

However, tiered pricing presents several challenges. If higher tiers lack perceived value, users may feel overcharged, leading to dissatisfaction. It is critical to price each tier appropriately, taking into account user expectations, market trends, and competition. Overpricing can drive users to competitors, while underpricing can reduce revenue and perceived value. In addition, maintaining consistent service quality across tiers can be costly, especially when differentiation between tiers is difficult. To be successful, FinTech companies must clearly communicate the value of each tier and ensure that users understand the benefits of upgrading. Striking a balance between affordability, transparency, and competitiveness is essential to maximize profitability and user satisfaction. Effectively demonstrating the benefits of higher tiers while maintaining reasonable pricing for lower tiers will drive conversions and increase perceived value.

CHAPTER 3

Payment Services

Abstract This chapter examines the growing role of payment services in FinTech sector, focusing on innovations in digital payments, remittances, and the impact of PSPs. The digitization of payment methods has led to significant advances in card technologies, digital wallets, and mobile POS systems, all designed to meet the growing demand for convenience, security, and speed. In addition, the chapter explores regulatory compliance and emerging technologies, such as QR code payments, payment gateways, and payment orchestrations. It illustrates how FinTech is enhancing traditional banking by improving the efficiency and accessibility of global financial transactions.

Keywords Payment accounts · Money transfers · Prepaid card issuing · POS · Digital wallets

A payment service is the process of sending money from one party to another. These services can be accessed through a variety of methods, including payment accounts, cards, and digital wallets. Technology is revolutionizing the payments industry by challenging traditional payment tools and institutions through digital innovation. The digitization of financial services has spurred FinTech innovation, resulting in more efficient, secure, and user-friendly payment solutions. In addition, new

T. Geçer and V. Akgiray, *The Financial Technology Revolution*,
https://doi.org/10.1007/978-3-031-92048-6_3

entrants to the payments market are introducing innovative solutions that compete with traditional banking tools (Carstens, 2020).

Four key trends have driven the expansion of digital payment services. The pandemic accelerated the transition from cash to contactless payments, a shift that was already underway. Payment services experienced significant growth, largely due to government initiatives promoting cashless transactions to increase interoperability, combat tax evasion, improve aid distribution, and facilitate adoption (Puzhakkal & Sivansankaran, 2024). The global rise in e-commerce has further increased the volume of transactions. Regulatory oversight is critical for digital payments, which require approvals, permits, and licenses. By law, only banks, e-money institutions, and payment institutions are authorized to operate as PSPs and must comply with applicable regulations, industry standards, and international security protocols.

3.1 Payment Accounts

PSPs specialize in opening, managing, and maintaining payment accounts, providing secure, seamless, and integrated financial services to ensure accessibility for all users. These accounts allow users and businesses to track transactions, manage funds, and make deposits and transfers using payment cards, bank accounts, and other financial instruments. In addition, payment accounts facilitate convenient purchases on e-commerce platforms, online marketplaces, and physical retail stores. The company operating the Payment Account Platform is FinTech.

Payment Account Service Revenues

PSPs typically generate revenue through subscription fees and pay-per-use fees for transactions such as deposits, withdrawals, transfers, and purchases. Additional revenue streams include currency conversion fees, foreign exchange spreads, and chargeback and cancelation fees. PSPs also cater to high-volume businesses, such as e-sports, gaming, and betting platforms, and charge higher commission rates. In addition, some PSPs monetize APIs by charging companies for access to their payment infrastructure and data integration services.

3.2 Money Transfers

Money transfer is the process of transferring money from one party to another, typically involving three key steps: sending, clearing, and settlement. The company operating the Money Transfer Platform is FinTech.

Figure 3.1 shows all possible directions of money transfers between different parties.

Types of Money Transfers

M2M:	A person or business transfers money to their account.
P2P	A person transfers money to another person's account.
P2B	A person transfers money to a business account.
P2G	A person transfers money to a government account.
B2G	A business transfers money to a government account.
B2B	A business transfers money to another business's account.
B2P	A business transfers money to a person's account.

Money Transfer Service Revenues

Money transfer revenue is primarily derived from fees charged to users for international money transfers. This includes a service fee, an exchange margin and the difference between the company's rates and the market rates (WorldRemit, 2021). Additional revenue streams may include fees for instant transfers, corporate services such as payroll and vendor payments, advertising revenue from third-party brands, interest earned on invested account balances, and partnerships with banks, card schemes, and other financial institutions.

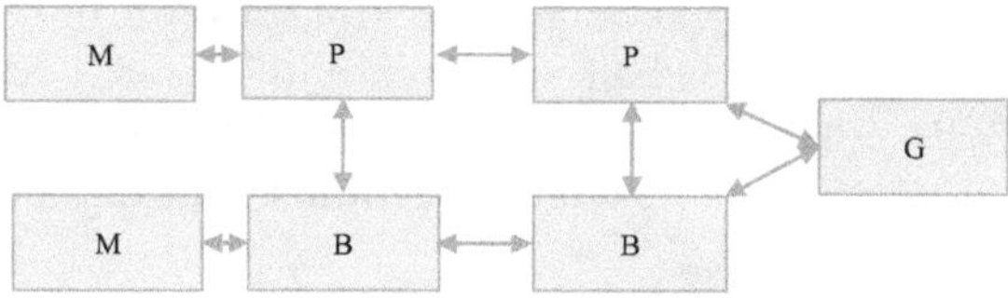

Fig. 3.1 Types of money transfers

Case Study 3.1: Wise

Wise, formerly known as TransferWise, is a London-based FinTech specialized in international money transfers and cross-border payments. Founded in 2011, the company has quickly become a global leader in digital payments. By establishing a network of local banks around the world, Wise facilitates seamless transactions and ensures faster, safer, and more reliable transfers (KPMG, 2017).

Wise operates on a P2P currency exchange system, eliminating traditional bank fees, and offering competitive exchange rates at a lower cost. Unlike banks that add markups to exchange rates, Wise uses only the mid-market rate with no hidden fees. Its pricing structure is completely transparent, consisting of a small percentage-based fee along with a fixed per-transaction fee, ensuring clarity and fairness for users.

Wise's Products

Wise Platform is a global payments infrastructure designed for banks, financial institutions, and corporations. It provides network necessary to facilitate fast, secure, and cost-effective international payments directly within their platforms. By providing a seamless and scalable solution for managing cross-border transactions, Wise Platform enables businesses to expand internationally while ensuring efficiency and transparency (Wise, 2024).

Wise has revolutionized the international remittance industry by providing an affordable, transparent, and easy-to-use alternative to traditional banking services. With a strong emphasis on innovation and user-centric solutions, Wise has positioned itself as a key player in the global financial markets. Its commitment to improving the efficiency and accessibility of cross-border transactions continues to drive its growth and success.

3.3 Payment Card Acquiring

PSPs enable merchants to accept credit, debit, and prepaid cards by providing secure and efficient payment processing services. They manage the processing, storage, and transmission of cardholder and authentication data on behalf of other entities (PCI SSC, 2024b). In addition, PSPs provide the infrastructure to support multiple payment methods, including cards, payment accounts, and digital wallets, ensuring smooth

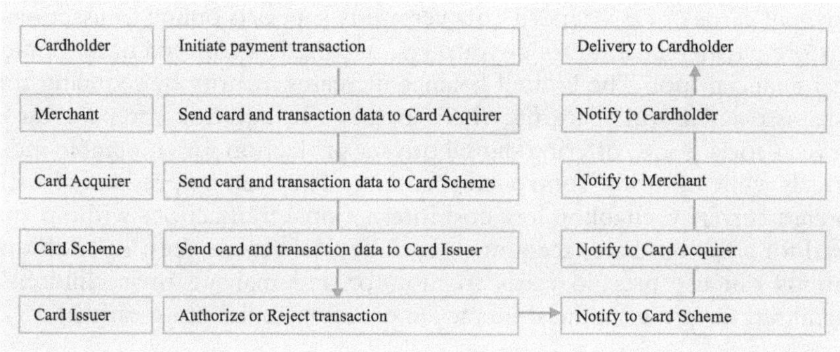

Fig. 3.2 Payment card authorization flows

transaction processing and settlement. PSPs adhere to strict international security standards to protect user data and prevent fraud. Payment transactions typically follow three essential steps: authorization, clearing, and settlement. For card transactions, authorization occurs when card acquirer verifies the transaction with card issuer or processor (PCI SSC, 2018). Beyond these core services, PSPs may provide additional support, including chargeback management, dispute resolution, call center services, and cardholder support.

Figure 3.2 illustrates payment card authorization process, detailing the data flow, authorizations, and notifications among key stakeholders.

3.4 Prepaid Card Issuing

Prepaid cards, issued by banks or PSPs (non-banks), allow cardholders to make payments and purchases up to their available balance. These cards offer several key benefits, including enhanced privacy through cardholder anonymity and improved spending control by limiting purchases to card's balance. Prepaid cards are available in both physical (plastic) and virtual (card number) formats to meet user preferences. Prepaid cards promote financial inclusion by providing access to financial services for unbanked and underbanked. Because they do not have a credit limit, these cards remain accessible to individuals with limited or poor credit histories. Businesses also use prepaid cards for expense management, allowing employers to effectively monitor and control employee spending. Adding funds to a prepaid card is easy and flexible, with options including bank transfers, payment cards or cash deposits. Its versatility supports online transactions, in-store payments, and money transfers, making it a convenient and practical financial tool. The limited balance increases security by reducing the risks associated with hacking, theft, or loss. In addition, prepaid cards serve as social tools, offering digital privacy protection for vulnerable individuals while ensuring controlled spending. They can be pre-loaded with foreign currency, enabling low-cost international transactions without the need for a foreign bank account or currency conversion fees. In addition, parents can use prepaid cards to monitor and manage their children's spending, fostering financial literacy and responsibility at an early age.

Prepaid Card Revenues

Prepaid card revenue is generated through a variety of channels. PSPs can charge cardholders a subscription fee for card use and earn interchange fees from card acquirers when transactions are made at POS terminals. Prepaid cards are often the primary payment method on e-sports, gaming, and betting platforms. PSPs may also charge fees for reloading prepaid cards and for issuing both physical and virtual cards. Other revenue streams include currency conversion fees, foreign exchange margin gains, and cash transaction fees. PSPs may also offer additional services such as bill payment, payroll processing and programmable payments. Partnerships with merchants, banks, and card schemes also provide additional revenue opportunities.

3.5 Payment Initiation Services

These services allow users to make payments through a single platform, eliminating the need to access multiple banks or PSPs. Payment initiation services are particularly useful for recurring and programmable payments. Payment initiation service providers offer online services that initiate payment orders on behalf of users from a payment account held with another PSP (Open Banking, 2024). PSPs must obtain user consent before initiating transactions.

Payment initiation services offer a number of benefits. Users can track and manage their spending in real-time and receive instant notifications of pending, completed or unauthorized transactions. These services facilitate instant payments and transfers, reducing manual entry errors and minimizing the risk of late payments. By centralizing access to multiple accounts-including payment cards, bank accounts, and payment accounts-users can efficiently manage transactions on a single platform. In addition, consolidating financial information enhances both privacy and security. Users also have the ability to modify, reschedule, or cancel transactions as needed, providing greater flexibility and control. The company operating the Payment Initiation Platform is FinTech.

3.6 Account Information Services

These services aggregate financial data from bank accounts, payment accounts, and payment cards into a single platform, allowing users to view, monitor, and manage all of their accounts in one place without having to log in to multiple platforms. Account Information Service Providers consolidate financial data from users' accounts with one or more PSPs (Open Banking, 2024). PSPs must obtain user consent before initiating this service. These PSPs facilitate supreme financial management by providing users with unified access to all their accounts, payment cards, loans, investments, and insurance products from a single platform. This capability enables real-time financial monitoring, allowing users to track transactions, check balances and receive instant notifications of pending, completed or unauthorized transactions anytime, anywhere. The company operating the Account Information Platform is FinTech.

Payment Initiation and Account Information Service Revenues

PSPs generate revenue by providing payment initiation and account information services through various channels. They charge users subscription fees and pay-per-use fees for transaction processing, which includes both payment initiation and account information services. In addition, PSPs benefit from currency conversion, foreign exchange bid-ask spreads, chargebacks, reversals, and APIs. Value-added services such as robo-advisory, budgeting tools, and insurance provide additional monetization opportunities. Upselling and cross-selling strategies and data monetization enable PSPs to analyze user behavior, spending habits and preferences to improve service offerings and increase revenue. Strategic partnerships with banks, card schemes and merchants expand revenue streams through referral services and co-branded financial solutions.

Case Study 3.2: Fast

FAST (Instant and Continuous Transfer of Funds), an advanced instant payment system developed by the Central Bank of the Republic of Türkiye, was launched on January 8, 2021. It enables secure, fast, and seamless transactions around the clock, introducing an innovative approach to payments in Türkiye. Rapidly gaining acceptance, FAST is emerging as a robust alternative to cash and card payments for purchase transactions (CBRT, 2024).

Key features include:

- 24/7 Availability: Transactions are available anytime, including weekends and holidays.
- Instant Transfers: Transactions are completed within seconds, ensuring immediate access to funds.
- Flexible Limits: Banks adjust transaction limits based on current economic conditions.
- QR Code Payments: Users can make instant payments by scanning QR codes.
- User-Friendly Interface: Designed for simplicity, making it accessible to individuals with limited financial literacy.
- Financial Inclusion: Expands access to financial services for unbanked and underbanked population.
- Cost-Effective: Lower transaction fees offer benefits for both individuals and businesses.
- Seamless Interbank Transactions: Facilitates seamless transfers between participating banks.
- Robust Security: Backed by the Central Bank of the Republic of Türkiye, ensuring a secure payment environment.
- FinTech Integration: Supports digital wallets and mobile banking applications, encouraging financial innovation.

3.7 POS Services

PSPs provide merchants with POS services that enable secure and efficient payment acceptance, processing, clearing and settlement. These services enhance merchants' operations by providing a comprehensive payment infrastructure. POS systems can be divided into two main types.

- Physical POS: Hardware-based terminals that process transactions using payment cards, QR codes, or NFC-enabled mobile devices. These systems typically include card readers, printers, and network connectivity.
- Software POS: Web-based or app-based solutions that facilitate e-commerce checkout, online transactions, and digital wallet services.

Each system addresses different merchant needs. Physical POS systems support in-store and outdoor payments and enable direct interaction with cardholders, while software POS systems facilitate online checkout and digital transactions. The company operating the POS Platform is FinTech.

Type of POS

Physical POS

Physical POS terminals are advanced devices that integrate payment processing capabilities with traditional cash register functions, providing full POS functionality and receipt printing. Key feature of these terminals is their built-in fiscal memory, which securely stores transaction data for secure processing. These terminals help merchants streamline record-keeping, reporting and tax compliance, while increasing transaction speed and accuracy, which ultimately leads to improved user satisfaction. Portable mobile POS systems are compact versions of traditional terminals that allow merchants to process transactions from virtually anywhere, providing greater flexibility and convenience for mobile sales and payments. Both physical POS systems offer several benefits. They process payment cards quickly and facilitate cash transactions through an integrated cash register. Designed for indoor and outdoor use, these systems are compatible with peripherals such as scanners, card readers, printers, and traditional cash registers. They also interface with billing, sales, and inventory management systems, allowing merchants to monitor and manage their operations efficiently.

Physical POS devices meet international standards for fraud prevention and secure transactions. Their value proposition emphasizes speed, convenience, and increased user satisfaction and loyalty. These systems facilitate face-to-face transactions and can operate offline during network disruptions. They also generate detailed sales reports and provide insight into spending patterns, improving checkout efficiency, and reducing abandonment rates. POS systems continue to drive retail growth. Companies that deploy them see increased sales, while users report overwhelmingly positive experiences. The future of POS will be shaped by innovation, emerging technologies, and data-driven insights as businesses prioritize user intelligence and service enhancements to drive retail expansion (Barclays, 2018).

Digital POS

dPOS is a software-based physical POS device designed for indoor, outdoor, and mobile use. It provides efficient sales reporting and POS insights through an intuitive dashboard. As a cloud-based platform, dPOS ensures continuous accessibility and secure protection of payment data while collecting valuable information to analyze user spending patterns. It also provides essential business services such as inventory management, pre-accounting, and billing. With built-in communication tools, dPOS increases user satisfaction and loyalty. It integrates with digital wallets and NFC-enabled mobile devices for transactions. Remote updates and upgrades facilitate collaboration with banks, card schemes, and merchants. Its versatile design adapts to different environments, while its scalable architecture supports feature expansion and multi-location deployment.

Mobile POS

mPOS is a payment solution that allows merchants to process transactions using mobile devices or smartphones equipped with card readers. Key advantage of mPOS is its cost-effectiveness compared to traditional POS systems. By turning smartphones into payment terminals, mPOS increases flexibility and convenience. It speeds up user service, especially during peak hours and high traffic situations, reducing waiting times and increasing user satisfaction and loyalty. In addition, mPOS provides remote access to payment and transaction data, streamlining billing, sales, and inventory management. Its easy configuration and automatic updates minimize the learning curve for staff. Compact and versatile, mPOS is suitable for indoor, outdoor, and mobile use. Its scalable design supports business growth and ensures long-term efficiency as operational needs evolve.

SoftPOS

sPOS is payment software that turns NFC-enabled smartphones into payment terminals, eliminating the need for physical card readers. This secure and easy-to-use technology is ideal for small businesses and mobile merchants. sPOS allows merchants to accept payments anywhere and supports multiple methods, including credit and debit cards, digital wallets, QR codes, and NFC-enabled devices. By eliminating the need for physical hardware, sPOS reduces upfront investment and lowers overall infrastructure costs. Compliant with international security standards, sPOS protects sensitive user data. It is easy to set up and update, making it scalable for growing businesses. In addition, sPOS provides valuable business intelligence insights to track sales trends and manage inventory efficiently.

Virtual POS

vPOS is a web-based payment solution that provides browser access to acquirers, processors, and third-party service providers for payment card transaction authorization (PCI DSS, 2024). Users manually enter payment card information through a secure web interface. Commonly used by e-commerce and online platforms, vPOS operates as a web service or mobile application accessible from any digital device. It instantly processes card, account, and digital wallet payments, optimizing sales, inventory, and cash management. vPOS is easy to deploy and integrates with existing platforms, enabling merchants to process payments anytime, anywhere. Compliant with international standards, vPOS ensures secure data transmission. It also automates billing, streamlines checkout process, and supports multiple payment methods to facilitate global expansion. Cost-effective, vPOS reduces the marginal cost of payment processing.

POS Service Revenues

PSPs generate multiple revenue streams from POS services. They charge merchants a subscription fee for access to POS system and generate revenue from merchant discounts on payment card processing fees. In addition, foreign exchange gains contribute to their overall revenues. PSPs also generate revenue by selling physical POS terminals, peripherals, replacement parts and accessories, and by providing maintenance and repair services. Offering warranties and insurance for POS terminals further expands their revenue opportunities. In addition, PSPs can charge for POS software installation, updates, upgrades, security, and ongoing maintenance. Partnerships with banks, card schemes and third-party service providers create additional revenue streams.

Case Study 3.3: Square

Square, a subsidiary of Block Inc., was launched in February 2009 as part of Block's broader ecosystem. It provides POS and payment services that enable merchants to accept card payments via smartphones, tablets, or terminals. Before companies like Square, small businesses faced high fees and complicated equipment to process card transactions. Square simplifies payment processing, allowing businesses to accept payments, print receipts, and offer virtual gift cards to users (Columbia Engineering, 2024).

Over time, Square has evolved into a comprehensive commerce ecosystem, offering more than 30 products that help businesses manage their operations through a unified platform. One of Square's key strengths is its scalability; merchants can begin with basic functionality and expand to more advanced features as their needs evolve. This flexibility allows merchants to adapt and scale efficiently.

<u>Some of Square Products</u> (Block Inc., 2024)

- Square for Restaurants: Dedicated solution for both quick and full service restaurants.
- Square Appointments: Comprehensive solution for appointment-based businesses that integrates reservation capabilities with POS functionality.
- Square for Retail: Solution specifically designed for retail merchants.
- Square POS: Versatile POS application that can be customized to meet the needs of various merchants at different stages of business development.
- Square Online: Platform designed for creating websites and online stores, featuring integration for selling on Instagram and Facebook.
- Square Online Checkout: Tool for creating simple checkout links for online sales without requiring a full website.
- Square Billing: Customizable billing solution that offers secure online payment processing.
- Square Virtual Terminal: Solution that allows merchants to use a computer as a POS terminal.

3.8 Digital Wallets

Digital wallets allow users to store funds and conduct transactions. These applications securely store payment credentials and are accessible through smartphones, smartwatches, tablets, computers, and terminals, providing both convenience and security (Worldpay, 2023). The company operating the Digital Wallet Platform is FinTech.

Figure 3.3 shows various sources of funds for digital wallets, including credit cards, debit cards, prepaid cards, bank accounts, cash, e-money, and other payment accounts.

Digital wallets are increasingly integrated into various ecosystems and woven into users' daily lives through sectors such as e-commerce, ride-hailing, food delivery, messaging, and travel. These wallets facilitate fast transactions while providing account monitoring, budgeting, and expense management capabilities. They support a wide range of financial transactions, including P2P, A2A, B2B, and domestic and international remittances. By consolidating multiple payment methods into a single platform, digital wallets enable QR code payments and are compatible with NFC-enabled devices. The ease-of-use of digital wallets is a key factor driving their adoption and continued popularity (Khasawneh & Al-Bahsh, 2024).

3.8.1 Types of Digital Wallets

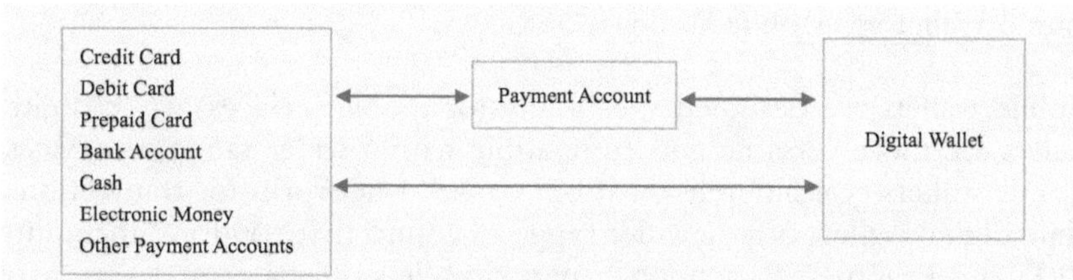

Fig. 3.3 Digital wallets

Pass-Through Digital Wallets

Pass-through digital wallets transmit tokenized payment credentials to the seller, who processes the transaction directly with their acquirer (Visa, 2024b). These wallets do not store funds; rather, they facilitate payments by securely transmitting credentials to merchant and allowing users to select their preferred payment method. This approach increases security and convenience for users while ensuring efficient transactions for merchants.

Stored-Value Digital Wallets

This assigns a separate account to user, which they preload with funds using their payment credentials prior to making transactions on the digital wallet platform (Visa, 2024b). User maintains a dedicated payment account that holds transferred funds during transactions, enhancing security and ensuring seamless payments. Users authenticate their identity using verifiable methods such as passwords or fingerprints; however, the payment method is not issued by the PSP associated with card or account (U.S. Payments Forum, 2018).

Stage Digital Wallets

These wallets do not store funds. Instead, users register their payment methods in advance, and funds are only transferred to the payment account during transactions. The wallet acts as a temporary holding space rather than a long-term storage solution and is often used for promotional offers or unique conveniences (Kamal et al., 2023). This approach streamlines payments while increasing user flexibility and efficiency.

Digital Wallet vs. Mobile Wallet

Mobile wallets are designed specifically for mobile devices, while digital wallets are more versatile and compatible with a wider range of devices. Mobile wallets typically rely on Wi-Fi or GSM networks for transactions, while digital wallets offer a wider range of connectivity options, including Wi-Fi and Ethernet. Functionally, digital wallets offer a greater variety of features, while mobile wallets are streamlined for basic tasks on mobile devices. Design differences reflect these functionalities: mobile wallets have compact interfaces and simplified menus optimized for smaller screens and limited memory. In contrast, digital wallets use larger screens and more extensive menus to accommodate complex transactions and enhance user experience.

Advantages of Digital Wallets

Digital wallets offer several benefits, including cash management, budgeting tools, and expense tracking, all in a single platform. They typically charge lower fees than alternative payment methods and comply with international security standards to ensure robust data protection. As an integrated solution, digital wallets also support loyalty programs, such as airline miles and store rewards (JP Morgan, 2021). The privacy and data security features of digital wallets can vary, similar to the differences between credit and debit cards. In addition, they operate under different legal frameworks regarding disclosure of terms and conditions, liability for unauthorized transactions, and error resolution (Levitin, 2017).

Disadvantages of Digital Wallets

Digital wallets have several drawbacks. Despite their growing prevalence and impact, they offer significant societal benefits while facing unresolved privacy and legal issues (Turi, 2023). Users may face accessibility issues when relying on a single device, as malfunctions, low battery life, or unavailability can disrupt transactions. In addition, slow Internet connections can hinder payment processing. Security remains a major concern, as consolidating multiple payment methods into a single platform makes digital wallets prime targets for security breaches. In addition, not all merchants accept digital wallets, and some may charge additional fees for processing payments. Technological incompatibilities can arise when digital wallets do not integrate with all payment terminals. Regular software and security updates are critical, so users need to stay informed to ensure secure usage. In addition, non-technical users may struggle with the learning curve associated with using digital wallets effectively and securely.

Digital Wallet Revenues

PSPs generate multiple revenue streams from digital wallets, including subscription fees, transaction fees for payments and remittances, and currency conversion fees or profits from foreign exchange bid-ask spreads. Digital wallets are expanding their monetization strategies by entering new areas such as bill payments, merchant services, and remittances (McKinsey, 2022b). They can also charge additional fees for handling disputes, chargebacks, cancelations, and invest their account balances in money markets to earn interest. Opportunities for up-selling and cross-selling further increase revenue potential. Beyond transaction fees, digital wallets significantly impact the economics of payment cards and the flow of payment data. User data, a valuable by-product of transactions, is increasingly being integrated into monetization strategies (Levitin, 2017). PSPs can analyze user behavior and preferences to deliver targeted advertising to banks, card schemes, and merchants. They can also offer referral services to these entities, charge interchange fees to card acquirers, and generate revenue from APIs.

3.9 QR Payments

QR payments generate unique QR codes for each transaction, simplifying the payment process. QR codes are two-dimensional barcodes that store more information than traditional barcodes and can be scanned more quickly. There are two types of QR codes: merchant-presented and customer-presented.

Merchant-Presented QR Code

Merchants use QR codes to initiate payments, allowing customers to scan the code and complete transactions (World Bank Group, 2021). This method provides instant, secure payments and improves transaction speed, particularly during peak times. It serves as a cost-effective alternative to traditional payment methods. To implement QR payments, merchants must establish the necessary technical infrastructure, which includes a QR code generation system, a secure POS setup from a PSP, and compliance with global security standards to protect transactions and user data.

Customer-Presented QR Code

Customers generate QR codes that merchants scan to complete transactions (World Bank Group, 2021). This customer-presented payment method gives users more control by allowing them to generate and authorize payments. To use this method, users need a dedicated mobile app with Wi-Fi or GSM connectivity. In addition, users must pre-register a preferred payment method, such as a credit card, digital wallet, or bank account.

Advantages of QR Code Payments

QR code payments offer several benefits, including advanced security features that meet international standards to ensure secure transactions. They also provide valuable data and analytics for sales and POS transactions, providing insight into spending patterns. As a low-cost technology, QR codes offer easy user experience for both the presenter and the scanner (US FPC, 2022). QR code mobile payment services are faster, easier, and more secure than other mobile payment options, making them widely accepted, especially in technologically advanced societies (Liu et al., 2021). They enable quick and flexible payments in a variety of environments-indoors, outdoors, or on the move. In addition, QR code payments eliminate the need for plastic cards, increasing user convenience.

Disadvantages of QR Code Payments

QR code payments have several limitations. The lack of standardization and interoperability in QR code Specifications can negatively impact user experience. Because different vendors use different QR code formats, users may need multiple applications to transact with different merchants (World Bank Group, 2021). In addition, these payments require a smartphone or mobile device with the necessary capabilities, which excludes individuals who do not have access to such technology or are unfamiliar with smartphones. Technical issues or system glitches can disrupt transactions, resulting in a poor user experience. Proper use of QR codes is essential, as errors in scanning or code generation can result in incomplete or inaccurate transactions. Factors such as ambient lighting, camera quality, and scanning angle have a significant impact on the success of these transactions. Despite the growing adoption of QR code payments, not all merchants accept them, limiting their effectiveness in industries where mobile payments are not widely accepted.

QR Code Service Provider

QR code service providers, such as PSPs, specialize in QR code-based payment solutions. Their services include QR code generation, payment processing, clearing and settlement facilitation. They also offer analytics, reporting tools, payment system consulting and merchant support. These providers ensure compliance with international security standards while providing cost-effective solutions tailored to merchants' needs. They also incorporate branding elements into QR codes for marketing purposes and generate secure, tokenized, dynamic QR codes. The company operating the QR Code Platform is FinTech.

3.9.1 Payment Gateways

A payment gateway is a merchant service that authorizes and processes business transactions (Schueffel, 2017). It securely authenticates and transmits payment data between banks, card schemes, and PSPs, enabling credit and debit card payments. The rise in e-commerce has increased the demand for secure and flexible gateways that support multiple payment methods, currencies, and international transactions. In addition, the growing adoption of alternative payment options such as BNPL and EMI is reshaping user expectations and prompting merchants to offer a variety of payment solutions. Payment gateways streamline merchant transactions by integrating multiple PSPs into a single platform, simplifying the management of complex payment flows. Direct connections to banks, card schemes and PSPs increase efficiency, especially for high-volume merchants. The company operating the Payment Gateway Platform is FinTech.

Figure 3.4 summarizes the combinations of payment tools used in the payment gateway.

Payment gateways provide a variety of secure methods for merchants to accept payments while protecting sensitive information, significantly reducing the risk of potential POS system breaches (MasterCard, 2018). These gateways support foreign currency transactions and cross-border payments, extending merchants' global reach. They comply with security standards and provide tools to effectively monitor and manage payment

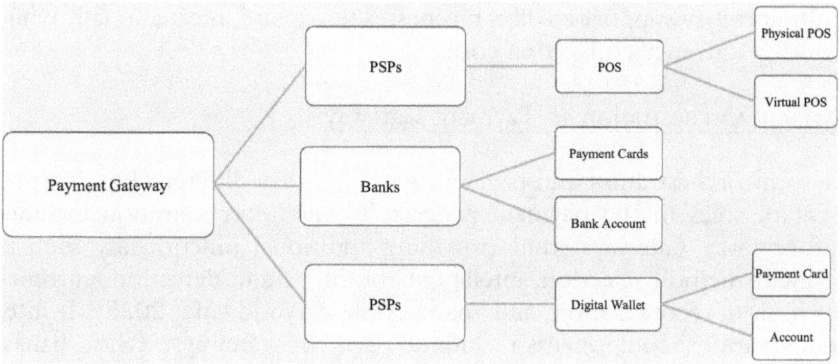

Fig. 3.4 Payment gateway

flows. By minimizing initial investment, working capital, and operational costs, payment gateways increase short-term user satisfaction and promote long-term user retention. However, there are some drawbacks to consider. Per-transaction fees can accumulate over time, negatively impacting profitability. In addition, some gateways may impose restrictions on supported payment methods and currencies, which can limit merchant's flexibility.

3.9.2 Payment Orchestration

Payment orchestration centralizes payment gateways, processors, acquirers, and other financial service providers on a single platform (Stripe, 2024b). This advanced service integrates multiple payment gateways, PSPs, payment methods, and foreign currencies into a unified system, enabling merchants to expand globally and meet diverse user needs. The company operating the Payment Orchestration Platform is FinTech.

Payment orchestration provides several benefits. It increases operational efficiency by streamlining payment processes and minimizing errors. Intelligent routing adapts payment gateways based on different scenarios, optimizing workflows. It also integrates with existing payment infrastructures, allowing merchants to quickly add new payment methods. Compliant with global security standards, payment orchestration enhances transaction security and protects user data. In addition, multi-currency support enables businesses to expand internationally while reducing currency conversion costs.

Payment Orchestration vs. Payment Gateway

Payment orchestration and payment gateways play different but complementary roles in the payment process. Payment orchestration includes one or more gateways while providing additional functionality such as payment method selection, intelligent routing, fraud detection, currency conversion, reconciliation, and analytics (ACI Worldwide, 2025). It integrates various components-including payment gateways, PSPs, banks, card schemes, and payment methods to create a comprehensive approach that enables merchants to efficiently manage complex payment ecosystems. In contrast, payment gateways focus on the technical aspects of payment processing.

A payment gateway acts as a bridge between payment processors, facilitating the transfer of funds between user and merchant accounts (ACI Worldwide, 2025). They encrypt or tokenize payment data, provide secure data transmission, and automate transaction routing. While payment gateways handle the mechanics of transactions, payment orchestration provides a broader framework that improves operational efficiency and user experience across multiple channels and payment methods.

Case Study 3.4: Fiserv

Fiserv, Inc. is a leading global payments and financial services company. Serving merchants, banks, credit unions, financial institutions, and corporations worldwide, Fiserv is committed to delivering best-in-class results. Its offerings include account processing, digital banking solutions, card processing, payments, e-commerce, card acquiring and processing, and the Clover cloud-based POS and business management platform (Fiserv, 2023a). Fiserv provides secure, innovative, and reliable technology solutions that enhance financial services experience.

Fiserv's diversified business model generates revenue from processing, licensing, subscription, and transaction-based fees, enabling merchants to effectively adapt to market changes. The company's broad product portfolio and robust market presence provide a competitive advantage and establish Fiserv as one of the largest and most profound players in payment industry. Despite technological disruption, regulatory pressures, and intense competition, Fiserv is well-positioned for growth, driven by its strong market position, diverse offerings, and ongoing commitment to innovation.

Programmable Payments Services by Fiserv (Fiserv, 2023b)

Programmable payments allow users to link multiple accounts and funding sources to a single payment card, simplifying money management. Users can access any linked account without having to remember the most appropriate funding source for each transaction. They can pre-select funding sources for specific categories or choose funding source at the time of the transaction. In addition, AI can recommend the optimal payment option, improving decision-making and optimizing cash flow.

CHAPTER 4

Payment Card Systems

Abstract This chapter provides a comprehensive analysis of global payment card systems, focusing on card schemes, payment processing, and the roles of card issuers, acquirers, and PSPs. It examines the mechanics of credit, debit, and prepaid cards, emphasizing their security features and widespread acceptance. The chapter discusses key technological advances, including EMV chip technology, contactless payments, tokenization, and the strategic influence of major card schemes such as Visa and MasterCard. It also explains regulatory compliance, card transactions, and clearing and settlement processes. The discussion also covers data protection standards, including PCI DSS, which protects payment data and ensures secure and efficient global payment transactions.

Keywords Card schemes · Open loop · Semi-closed loop · Semi-open loop · Closed loop · Card issuing · Card acquiring · OnUs transactions · NotOnUs transactions · EMV · Card processing

4.1 Card Schemes

A card scheme is a structured technical and commercial arrangement that supports one or more card brands and provides the organizational, legal, and operational framework for their services (ECB, 2009). These

T. Geçer and V. Akgiray, *The Financial Technology Revolution*,
https://doi.org/10.1007/978-3-031-92048-6_4

schemes function as global payment networks that ensure fast, secure, and reliable card transactions. By managing the transfer of funds and information between banks, PSPs, merchants, and technology companies, card schemes oversee critical processes such as transaction authorization, clearing, and settlement. They play a vital role in the globalization and democratization of payment systems, supporting billions of payment cards issued by thousands of banks and PSPs and ensuring their acceptance by millions of merchants worldwide. In addition, card schemes create and maintain the technologies, standards and protocols that enable card-based transactions.

Despite the growing popularity of digital payments, card schemes continue to demonstrate resilience by integrating innovations such as contactless cards, virtual cards, digital wallets, QR payments, and payment accounts. Their continued success depends on their ability to adapt to technological advances and evolving user preferences, ensuring the seamless operation of card-based payment ecosystems.

- Interoperability: Card schemes enable banks and PSPs to issue and acquire payment cards for both domestic and international transactions, ensuring widespread acceptance and usability.
- Integrity: They maintain the integrity of payment card settlement process and support various corporate objectives (Visa, 2024a).
- Diversity: Card schemes support different business models and payment methods, providing a wide range of payment solutions.
- Clearing and Settlement: They process, clear, and settle transactions efficiently and accurately, ensuring smooth payment processing.
- Security: Card schemes use a multi-layered security framework that integrates cryptographic privacy methods to protect sensitive personal information (Visa, 2024a).
- Collaboration: They work together with merchants, banks, and PSPs to create a unified global payment system.
- Financial Strength: Strong capital structure and extensive global expertise enhance stability and market reach.
- Technology Leadership: Card schemes drive innovation by developing advanced payment technologies and value-added services that enhance the payments landscape.
- Rulemaking: They establish comprehensive rules, protocols, and standards for global payment systems, ensuring consistency across various platforms.

Card Scheme Revenues

Card schemes generate revenue from several sources, including service fees, processing fees and value-added services. Service revenue is derived from fees based on total payment volume, providing a consistent revenue stream. Processing revenue includes fees for transaction authorization, clearing and settlement. In addition, card schemes generate revenue from value-added services such as issuing support, merchant acceptance solutions, risk management, identity verification, network access, and global transaction facilitation (Visa, 2024a). Revenues from these value-added services may be generated through fixed or transaction-based fees. These services, which may be integrated with the payment systems or offered separately, include security solutions, intelligence and data analytics, domestic and cross-border payments, payment processing, gateway services, and open banking solutions (MasterCard, 2023). Branding fees are charged for logo placement on payment cards and platforms, allowing issuers and merchants to leverage the credibility of established payment schemes. Technology and software services revenue comes from installations, upgrades, AI-driven algorithms, mobile payment applications, tokenization, and authentication solutions. The monetization of analytics and data provides an additional revenue stream. In addition, card schemes collect and report insights from their network of cardholders, merchants, banks, and PSPs, providing valuable information on spending patterns, transaction timing and geographic trends.

Case Study 4.1: Visa
Visa provides payment processing services for both Visa-branded and non-Visa-branded card transactions. In addition, Visa provides gateway routing services to other payment schemes. At the client's request, Visa may perform authorization, clearing, or settlement on its network either before or after the transaction is routed. In these cases, Visa earns data processing revenue for certain services (Visa, 2024a). For Visa-branded card transactions, Visa manages the authorization, clearing, and settlement processes and generates revenue from service fees, data processing, international transactions, and other sources.

Visa partners with banks and PSPs worldwide to issue Visa-branded credit, debit, and prepaid cards. These issuers are responsible for managing cardholder accounts, including setting credit limits, monitoring transactions, and providing customer service. Cardholders can obtain Visa cards either online or at physical bank branches. These cards facilitate purchases, ATM transactions, and day-to-day payment management. Merchants who accept Visa typically work with acquiring banks, or PSPs, which handle the technical and financial aspects of payment processing. Acquirers set up payment systems, process transactions and manage payment settlements for merchants.

Visa's global network is vital to the payments ecosystem, connecting cardholders, merchants, banks, and PSPs. Advanced security measures and fraud prevention technologies protect financial information and ensure secure transactions. Visa processes billions of transactions every day, offering fast authorization, clearing and settlement. The company continues to innovate by introducing contactless payments, digital wallets, and mobile payment solutions that improve convenience, speed, and security. These advancements strengthen Visa's position as a leader in global payments.

4.2 Payment Cards Matrix

Payment card system is as a two-sided market consisting of acquiring and issuing. These two sides support four different business strategies: open, semi-closed, semi-open, and closed loop. These models can be applied to different payment methods and instruments, including digital wallets, QR code payments and payment accounts.

Table 4.1 plots 16 business models for card acquiring and issuing.

4.2.1 Closed Loop Card Issuing

Closed loop refers to single-purpose payment cards (Fiserv, 2025). In this model, card issuers provide payment cards that are only valid at affiliated merchants, which has several advantages. First, these cards serve as a promotional tool, reinforcing issuer's brand and services. Second, they help retain users in card issuer's ecosystem by offering hyper-personalized services that foster loyalty and exclusivity, thereby increasing user engagement. Because payment cards generate significant revenue, the size of user base and merchant network has a direct impact on profitability. Closed loop cards allow issuers to better manage risk, streamline processing and

Table 4.1 Payment cards matrix

		Payment card acquiring			
		Open loop	*Semi-Closed loop*	*Semi-Open loop*	*Closed loop*
Payment card issuing	Open loop	1	2	3	4
	Semi-Closed loop	5	6	7	8
	Semi-Open loop	9	10	11	12
	Closed loop	13	14	15	16

integrate more efficiently with affiliated merchants. In addition, issuers retain ownership of all card-related data, providing precious insights into user behavior and spending patterns that enable targeted offers, marketing strategies, and data-driven decisions.

4.2.2 *Semi-Open Loop Card Issuing*

Card issuers provide valid payment cards to affiliated merchants and partner acquirers in a partially open model. There are several benefits to this approach. By partnering with banks and PSPs, issuers can expand their merchant reach and leverage collective expertise to gain a competitive advantage. Revenue-sharing agreements further enrich revenue streams and generate cash flow beyond a closed loop model. In addition, issuers can target specific market segments by partnering with specialized acquirers, such as those in airline industry, to offer co-branded cards. This model also effectively manages risk by ensuring card acceptance at affiliated merchants through trusted partner acquirers. By partnering with acquirers, issuers gain access to advanced technologies that enable innovative, customized services. Integration with partner payment systems improves user experience by streamlining transactions and personalizing offers to better meet user expectations.

4.2.3 *Semi-Closed Loop Card Issuing*

In this partially closed model, card issuers provide valid payment cards to all merchants except certain acquirers that do not meet certain criteria.

Issuers prefer this model for a number of reasons. It ensures compliance with regulations that restrict partnerships with acquirers that lack proper licensing, capitalization, or consumer protection measures. It also allows issuers to avoid acquirers with weak security and risk management capabilities, reducing potential vulnerabilities. This model also protects brand reputation by excluding acquirers with negative public perceptions. Finally, issuers may be reluctant to partner with competing card issuers, further influencing their decision to adopt semi-closed loop model.

4.2.4 Open Loop Card Issuing

In this model, card issuers provide payment cards that are accepted by all merchants. These cards are typically EMV-enabled, ensuring compatibility with any EMV-compliant payment system, and enabling frictionless transactions across multiple merchants. This widespread acceptance enables instant payments anywhere, increasing convenience and inclusiveness in the payments ecosystem. The model encourages innovation and competition, allowing issuers to differentiate their offerings with customized features, rewards, and incentives. By partnering with card acquirers, issuers can introduce value-added services and leverage payment data to personalize cardholder experience and drive targeted marketing. Open loop model's smooth integration with multiple payment systems emphases issuers' adaptability and commitment to innovation, enabling rapid entry into dynamic markets.

4.2.5 Closed Loop Card Acquiring

In this model, card acquirers enable affiliated merchants to accept only payment cards issued by themselves, which offers several advantages. First, it provides complete control over the payment process, thereby enhancing security and risk management. As the sole owners of payment card data, acquirers gain valuable insights into user behavior, preferences, and market trends, allowing them to offer more tailored services. Second, acquirers retain all merchant discount rates, eliminating the need to share revenue through interchange fees, which increases profitability and financial stability. Finally, by aligning their brand with specific industries, such as airlines or travel, acquirers can strengthen their marketing strategies and differentiate themselves from competitors.

4.2.6 Semi-Open Loop Card Acquiring

In this partially open model, card acquirers allow affiliated merchants to accept only payment cards issued by themselves and their partner card issuers. First, acquirers can control the payment process by accepting only cards that meet specific risk, security, and integrity standards. Working with leading card issuers improves merchant experience and facilitates industry-specific transactions. Second, exclusivity agreements allow acquirers to limit card acceptance to select partners, giving them access to premium users and strengthening their market position. By partnering with card issuers that specialize in retail, healthcare, education, transportation, and tourism, acquirers can effectively target these sectors. In addition, accepting only co-branded cards creates new business opportunities. Finally, acquirers can charge higher interchange fees on partner-issued cards, increasing their revenue potential.

4.2.7 Semi-Closed Loop Card Acquiring

In this partially closed model, card acquirers allow affiliated merchants to accept all payment cards except those issued by card issuers that do not meet certain criteria. Semi-closed model is a variation of the closed category, defined by the scope of the network on which card can be used (EC, 2018). Acquirers prefer this model for several reasons. First, it ensures regulatory compliance and facilitates a comprehensive risk assessment. Acquirers can refuse cards from issuers that do not comply with security standards or have been sanctioned, minimizing operational risk. In addition, acquirers can filter out high-risk transactions by assessing risk during card processing, improving overall system reliability. This model also allows acquirers to impose additional acceptance criteria while maintaining high processing standards. Finally, it gives acquirers greater autonomy and control over payment processes, strengthening their position in the payment ecosystem.

4.2.8 Open Loop Card Acquiring

In this open loop model, merchants affiliated with card acquirers accept all payment cards, which has several benefits. First, this model expands market reach, drives revenue growth, and encourages competition and innovation. Access to both domestic and international markets increases market penetration and attracts a diverse set of card acquirers, fostering continuous improvements in the payment system. Open loop model allows merchants to accept cards issued by any institution in the network, creating a more inclusive payment experience (Checkout, 2025). In addition, acquirers provide cost-effective payment solutions and ensure interoperability between different payment systems. This excellent payment processing creates network effects that attract more merchants and cardholders, further strengthening the system. Transaction data provides valuable insights into cardholder behavior, preferences, and market trends, enabling acquirers to optimize services and improve decision-making. Finally, open loop payments improve convenience, speed, accessibility, and sustainability (Visa, 2023).

Case Study 4.2: Starbucks Value Card

Starbucks Card is a branded stored-value card designed to provide users with a convenient payment method, facilitate gifting, and encourage frequent visits through Starbucks Rewards Program. These cards can be activated through various channels, including company-operated stores, most licensed locations, online at Starbucks.com, mobile devices, and third-party websites and locations (Starbucks, 2023). The primary purpose of Starbucks Card is to streamline payments while offering users discounts, coupons, and rewards earned by accumulating points through purchases at Starbucks (Munifa, 2022). User loyalty is influenced by the likelihood of repeat purchases and ongoing engagement with the company's services, such as the continued use of Starbucks Card (Maharani, 2023).

<u>Starbucks Closed Loop Model</u>

Starbucks Value Card operates as a closed loop system, restricting its use to Starbucks network, which includes physical stores, mobile app, and the online store. When linked to a Starbucks Rewards account, users earn Stars with every purchase, which can be redeemed for free beverages, food, or other rewards. Card features an auto-reload option that automatically replenishes low balances. This closed loop model increases user engagement and brand loyalty by directly associating card usage with Starbucks and encouraging repeat visits. It also allows Starbucks to track and analyze users' purchasing behavior to inform targeted marketing strategies and personalized promotions. In addition, when users load funds onto their Starbucks Card, the company receives cash upfront, even if funds remain unspent.

4.3 EMV

EMV is global payment standards for issuing and acquiring cards that ensures interoperability and security between payment systems (Schueffel, 2017). It enables all payment cards issued by EMVCo member banks and PSPs to be accepted by all merchants affiliated with those banks and PSPs. EMVCo, an international organization founded by major global card schemes such as Visa and MasterCard, oversees the development and management of all EMV technologies.

EMV Technologies

EMV technologies, governed by the EMV Specifications and Programs (EMVCo, 2024a), facilitate smooth and secure transactions by ensuring compatibility, security, efficiency, and interoperability among payment systems. These technologies emphasize the storage and processing of payment data while protecting transaction information. They provide a layered security framework designed to prevent fraud and unauthorized access, all while supporting contactless payments that enhance convenience and speed. EMV establishes security standards that ensure global acceptance and protection for billions of payment cards.

EMV Contact Chip Technology

EMV technology enables in-store chip card payments that require physical contact with a payment terminal (EMVCo, 2024b). This contact-based technology enhances both the security and convenience of payment cards and terminals. It provides dynamic data authentication and offline PIN verification, significantly strengthening payment security. In addition, EMV supports global acceptance, providing enhanced functionality and fraud protection for EMV-compliant cards.

EMV Contactless Chip Technology

EMV contactless chip technology enables fast and secure payment processing by integrating NFC capabilities with robust security features. It is governed by the EMV Chip, EMV Contactless and EMV Contactless Kernel Specifications, which ensure smooth processing of contact and contactless transactions worldwide (EMVCo, 2024b). This technology uses advanced cryptographic algorithms, strong card authentication protocols, transaction monitoring, and comprehensive risk management strategies to enhance payment security.

EMV Mobile Technology

EMV technology enables secure and convenient contactless payments on mobile devices, including mobile wallets and card transactions on smartphones, tablets, and wearables via NFC (EMVCo, 2024b). By integrating secure elements and cloud-based storage, these devices act as efficient payment terminals while protecting sensitive information. EMV mobile technology supports both NFC and QR code payments, enabling seamless interoperability across platforms.

EMV Payment Tokenization Technology

EMV Tokenization enhances the security of digital payments by mitigating the risks associated with compromised or fraudulent use of PANs (EMVCo, 2024b). This technology protects sensitive payment data, including card numbers, expiration dates and verification codes, by replacing them with a unique token. Working in a layered security framework, EMV Tokenization reduces the risk of unauthorized access and strengthens overall payment security.

EMV QR Code Technology

EMV QR Code Specifications provide a standardized framework for generating QR codes, ensuring consistent platform functionality and enabling secure, reliable card-based and account-based payments (EMVCo, 2024b). These specifications make QR-based payments an efficient mobile payment solution for both users and merchants. EMV QR codes typically contain three key components:

- Merchant Information: This section identifies merchant and includes account information necessary for accurate payment processing.
- Transaction Information: This section identifies the payment amount, currency, and transaction type.
- Security Information: This includes cryptographic protocols and security measures specifically designed to protect the transaction.

EMV Secure Remote Commerce Technology

EMV SRC enhances the security and convenience of online shopping by streamlining checkout process while ensuring consistency and security for cardholders. It securely stores sensitive card data and enables seamless payment processing through advanced encryption and tokenization, creating a robust e-commerce framework. In addition, EMV SRC ensures compatibility across multiple platforms and devices, promoting interoperability in global payments ecosystem.

EMV 3 Domain Secure Technology

3D Secure protocol significantly reduces online card fraud and protects merchants from chargebacks associated with fraudulent transactions (US Payments Forum, 2018). It enhances the security of account-based transactions by protecting sensitive card data. Using advanced encryption and tokenization techniques, 3D Secure establishes a robust security framework for e-commerce checkout.

Case Study 4.3: EMVCo

Founded in 1999, EMVCo's mission is to combat card fraud, promote innovation, and enhance security within the payments industry (EMVCo, 2024a). Originally established by Europay, Mastercard, and Visa (EMV), it set the global standard for in-store smart card payments. American Express, Discover, and UnionPay later joined the consortium (Basin et al., 2021). EMVCo operates as a monopoly, ensuring global interoperability and secure acceptance of payment cards. It develops and manages EMV Specifications and testing processes to standardize payment technologies.

- EMV develops and maintains to ensure secure and interoperable payment solutions.
- EMV standardizes payment technologies, including contact and contactless transactions.
- EMV manages certification and testing programs to ensure compliance with security standards.
- EMV enhances payment security through the implementation of encryption, tokenization, and fraud prevention strategies.
- EMV facilitates global interoperability to enable smooth cross-border transactions.

4.4 Payment Card Issuing

Payment cards, including credit, debit, and prepaid cards, are widely accepted both domestically and internationally. Credit and debit cards are issued exclusively by banks, while prepaid cards can be issued by both banks and non-banks (PSPs). Prepaid cards require cardholders to preload funds, while debit cards facilitate payments by deducting funds directly from user's bank account (Worldpay, 2023).

Credit cards, on the other hand, allow cardholders to make purchases up to a predetermined credit limit set by the issuing bank. If the balance is paid in full and on time, card functions similarly to a charge card. However, any unpaid balance accrues interest and effectively becomes a loan. As one of the fastest growing financial products, credit cards provide a simple credit service (Niu & Zheng, 2019). They are universally accepted because they provide quick access to funds, facilitate cashless transactions, and enhance security.

Figure 4.1 shows the characteristics of payment cards, including those issued by banks (credit, debit, and prepaid cards) and those issued by non-banks (prepaid card).

Payment card issuing revenues are divided into three main groups:

- Card Fees: Issuers charge fees for primary and additional cards, renewals, ATM transactions, cash withdrawals, and value-added services.

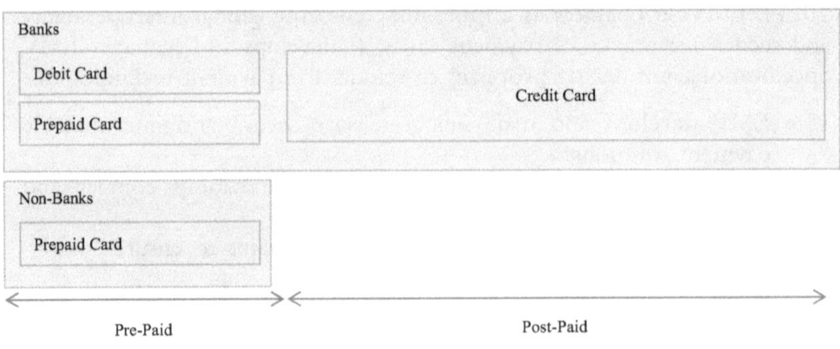

Fig. 4.1 Payment cards

Fig. 4.2 OnUs Transactions

- Interest Income: Issuers earn interest in cash advances, late fees, overdrafts, and installment plans.
- Interchange Fees: Issuers earn interchange fees when their cards are accepted by affiliated merchants of acquirer.

4.5 Payment Cards Acquiring

Payment Card Acquiring by Banks

Banks can provide payment card acquiring services acting as both PSP and credit institution.

There are four types of acquiring models.

4.5.1 OnUs Transactions

An OnUs transaction is a domestic transaction where card issuer and the acquirer are the same bank (MasterCard, 2024). In this model, bank acts as both card issuer and acquirer, enabling it to generate revenue from both sides of the transaction.

Figure 4.2 illustrates the revenue from OnUs Transactions.

4.5.2 NotOnUs Transactions 1 (Private Card Networks)

In this model, card issuer and acquirer are separate banks in a private card network set up by a leading bank or PSP. The network sets the interchange fees that card acquirer pays to card issuer. This structure encourages cooperation among participating banks and rules transactions. For example, Garanti BBVA (the leading bank of the Bonus network) unites eight domestic banks on Bonus platform (Bonus, 2025).

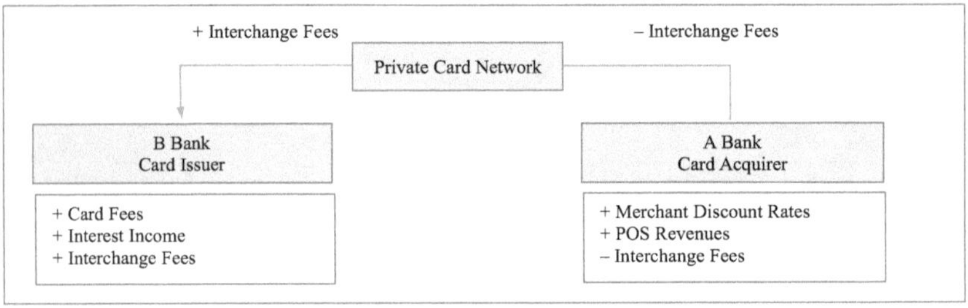

Fig. 4.3 NotOnUs Transactions 1 (Private Card Network)

Figure 4.3 illustrates the revenues, and the interchange fee flows in the private card network.

4.5.3 NotOnUs Transactions 2 (National Card Schemes)

In this model, card issuer and acquirer are separate banks operating in a national card scheme. This scheme sets the interchange fee that card acquirer pays to card issuer and encourages cooperation among national banks while regulating transaction. For example, BKM (Interbank Card Center) manages the authorization, clearing, and settlement processes for credit, debit, and prepaid cards, setting national rules and regulations to ensure standardization (BKM, 2025).

Figure 4.4 illustrates the revenues, and the interchange fee flows in the national card scheme.

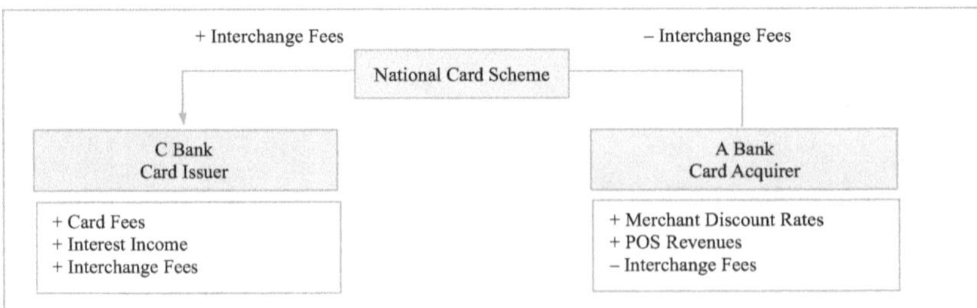

Fig. 4.4 NotOnUs Transactions 2 (National Card Scheme)

4.5.4 *NotOnUs Transactions 3 (International Card Schemes)*

In this model, card issuer and card acquirer are separate banks operating in different countries that participate in international card schemes such as Visa and MasterCard. Card schemes set the interchange fee that card acquirer pays to card issuer. This arrangement facilitates international transactions, standardizes fees, and ensures interoperability in the global payment system.

Figure 4.5 illustrates the revenues, and the interchange fee flows in the international card schemes.

Table 4.2 shows the flows of merchant discount rate, interchange fee, and scheme fee.

Payment Card Acquired by PSPs

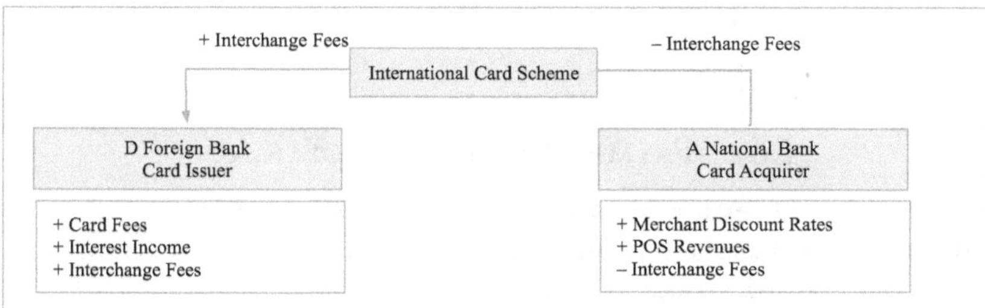

Fig. 4.5 NotOnUs Transactions 3 (International Card Schemes)

Table 4.2 Fee flows in card acquiring and issuing

	Cardholder	Merchant	Card Acquirer	Card Scheme	Card Issuer
Purchase	−100 →	+100			
Merchant Discount Rate		−6 →	+6		
Interchange Fee			−3 →	→	+3
Scheme Fee			−1 →	+1	
				+1 ←	−1
Clearing	−100	+94	+2	+2	+2

PSPs (non-banks) play a critical role in the payments ecosystem by offering several key benefits. One significant advantage is their ability to convert NotOnUs transactions into OnUs transactions, thereby eliminating interchange fees typically charged by card issuers. In addition, PSPs enable installment payments for all credit cards, allowing merchants to offer flexible payment options to their users.

Merchants benefit from accessing both physical and virtual POS systems through a single PSP, eliminating the need to purchase from multiple vendors. This approach streamlines the acquiring process and simplifies vendor management. PSPs also facilitate multi-POS connectivity and provide comprehensive technical support, reducing the administrative burden. In addition, a single agreement minimizes the legal burden on merchants. PSPs also provide maintenance, repairs, installations, and upgrades for both types of POS systems, ensuring secure and reliable transaction capabilities. By partnering with PSPs that adhere to international standards, merchants can increase the security of their transactions.

4.6 Payment Card Processing

Payment card processing involves many steps, from designing and manufacturing physical cards to managing and distributing them. The company operating the Card Processing Platform is FinTech.

4.6.1 Procurement of Raw Cards

The production of physical payment cards starts with raw, unpersonalized plastic cards that contain a magnetic stripe, a chip and various security features. Authorized manufacturers produce these cards according to the design and security specifications provided by card scheme or issuer. Each card is assigned a unique serial number for classification, traceability, and personalization.

Payment card personalization includes cardholder's name, card number, expiration date, and verification codes. Card design features can include vertical or horizontal orientation, materials such as plastic or metal, full-surface foils, colored edges, translucent elements, foil embossing, color-shifting inks, pearlescent inks, metallic inks, and textured finishes (Fiserv, 2020). Additional features such as holograms, special printing techniques, and security identifiers can also be integrated.

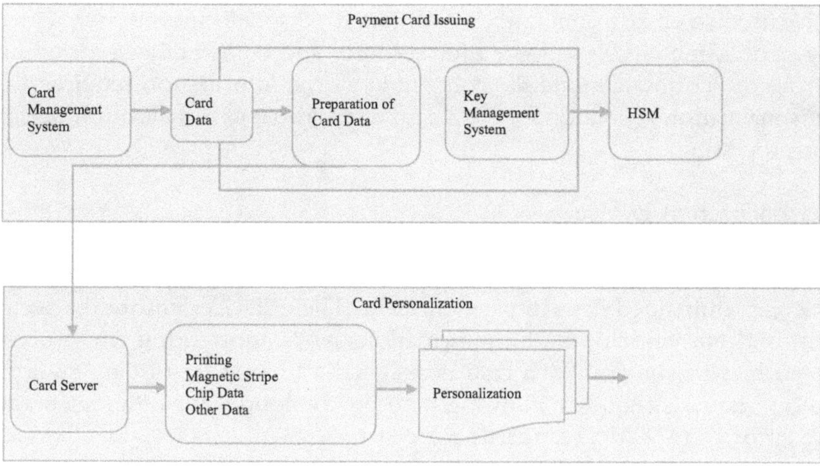

Fig. 4.6 Payment card personalization flow

Each card undergoes rigorous testing to ensure physical integrity, compliance with security standards, and the accuracy of all information. In addition to serving as a payment tool, these cards also serve as a branding, communications, and imaging tool for issuers. The quality and composition of cards have a significant impact on cardholder and merchant experience.

Figure 4.6 outlines payment card issuing and personalization process, highlighting key components such as card data preparation, encryption, key management, card server operations, and personalization steps.

4.6.2 Card Data Preparation

Card data preparation involves the secure management of information prior to payment card personalization, with an emphasis on encryption and secure key storage. Process begins by organizing the data on card chip, which includes cardholder's name, card number, expiration date, and verification code. Next, security keys and tokens required for secure transactions are generated. Data preparation rules define key generation, risk parameters, and data groupings presented to the terminal (Entrust, 2024). All sensitive information, including security keys, is encrypted to prevent unauthorized access. The encrypted data is then formatted to ensure compatibility with card personalization device. Once formatted, the data is validated for accuracy and completeness, including error corrections. Unique file containing all the information required for personalization is created for each card and sent to personalization device for processing.

Personalization Device

Personalization device transfers customized data from dedicated files to the chip embedded in each payment card. These devices ensure the accuracy and authenticity of the information, while monitoring the process to correct any errors. Each card is assigned a unique set of data tailored to card issuer's requests, allowing it to be configured for different usage scenarios and security standards.

Interaction with Personalization Devices and Smart Card

Effective card personalization is critical to protecting cardholder data and maintaining the integrity of payment card issuers. Personalization process ensures the accuracy and reliability of the data stored on card's chip by securely encoding settings such as PIN length, encryption keys, and security parameters. Proper configuration of these elements is critical to protecting cardholder data and facilitating secure transactions. The interaction between personalization devices and card must be seamless, with messaging protocols playing a critical role in enhancing security and maintaining data integrity. As a result, payment card industry has established strict data protection and messaging standards to ensure global acceptance and secure card usage.

Smart Card Applications

Card applications are essential for both functionality and security during personalization process. They securely receive data from personalization device and store it in card memory using encryption protocols. This ensures data integrity and authorized access.

4.6.3 *Personalization*

Advanced technology personalizes preprinted plastic cards by embedding account numbers and other identifying information (Mizen, 2016). Card personalization ensures that each smart card is unique, functional, and secure by encoding cardholder's identity, account information, and essential security features. Personalization process includes chip authentication, applet installation, data grouping, and card locking/key rotation (Entrust, 2024). Specialized machines implement these protocols to ensure reliable and secure card issuing.

Magnetic Stripe Personalization

Cardholder data is encoded on the magnetic stripe according to ISO Standards that specify its physical properties, including flexibility and dimensions.

Chip Personalization

Cardholder data, including name, card number, expiration date and verification codes, is uploaded to the chip for both contact and contactless transactions. This process also installs card's operating system, applications, and specific parameters. Once the chip is configured for user mode, its applications are activated, preventing further modification, ensuring secure storage, and controlling access to cardholder data. Personalization of contactless chips is carried out using special equipment designed for contactless functionality.

Card Surface Printing

Text and images are applied using inkjet printing, reverse transfer printing, laser engraving, and protective foils. Additional processes such as embossing, debossing, text coloring and scratch-resistant coatings enhance the durability and aesthetics of card. Branding and personalized labels can also be applied. Finally, quality assurance testing ensures compliance with industry standards.

4.6.4 *Hardware Security Module*

HSMs are specialized processors designed to secure cryptographic keys throughout their lifecycle. Essential for securing transactions, identities, and applications, HSMs manage keys while providing services such as encryption, decryption, authentication, and digital signatures (Thales, 2024b). They process PINs and PIN Blocks at ATMs and POS terminals, generate card verification codes, and create key sets for payment cards. In addition, HSMs conduct payment credentials for both cards and mobile applications, ensuring secure transactions in compliance with EMV Contact and Contactless Specifications.

4.6.5 *Plastic Card Delivery*

Processors manage the delivery of payment cards, overseeing entire process from personalization to secure distribution. Personalized cards are carefully packaged to prevent damage and ensure security. They are organized by recipient address and prepared for mailing, using postal and logistics services to ensure secure and timely delivery. Security measures, including tracking and monitoring, protect against unauthorized access during transit. Upon receipt, cardholders must activate their cards before use. They will receive detailed instructions on card usage, security precautions and activation process. In addition, support services are available to help cardholders as needed.

4.6.6 *Data Updates*

After issuing, data update process modifies a payment card's application data and security components to meet evolving needs and maintain current security standards. This process, managed by processors, integrates both physical and digital security protocols with payment cards that support remote data updates. Updates can include changes to personal information (such as cardholder name or account information), card numbers, security credentials (such as PIN or card verification codes), and card limits.

4.6.7 Chargeback

A chargeback is a refund issued by card issuer to cardholder for a disputed charge (Alt & Huch, 2022). The primary purpose of chargebacks is to protect cardholders from errors, unethical practices, and irregularities. Chargebacks adhere to the "cardholder first" principle, which encourages merchants to maintain fair and transparent practices.

There are several key steps in the chargeback process:

- Dispute: This process begins when cardholder disputes a charge with issuer. Disputes typically fall into one of seven categories: fraud, failure to receive goods or services, product quality issues, cancelations, failure to receive information, processing errors, or authorization issues (Hayashi et al., 2016).
- Process: After initiating dispute, card issuer forwards it to card acquirer, who contacts merchant for resolution.
- Accept or Deny: Merchants have the option of either accepting or denying a dispute. If they accept dispute, funds are transferred to cardholder's account and deducted from merchant's account. If they deny dispute, merchants must provide evidence to support their claim, which may lead to pre-arbitration or, if necessary, arbitration.

4.6.8 Customer Services

Payment card customer service provides a secure and user-friendly experience that helps issuers maintain a positive reputation. These services include blocking lost or stolen cards to prevent unauthorized use and financial loss. Cardholders can inquire about their credit, request balance updates, and apply for credit limit increases. Support services also help with PIN management, including setting, resetting, and changing PINs to ensure secure access. They also provide information on account balances and recent transactions and facilitate card activation and deactivation. Emergency services, such as issuing replacement cards, are also available. Ongoing transaction monitoring for suspicious activity is critical, with cardholders notified immediately of any anomalies. These services enhance security, convenience, and overall cardholder experience.

4.6.9 Clearing and Settlement

Clearing and settlement process entails the exchange of information between issuers and acquirers, calculation of final balances, and settlement of outstanding debts. Clearing includes transmission, reconciliation, and, in some cases, confirmation of transfer orders prior to settlement (ECB, 2009). During this process, transaction data is transmitted to card acquirer. Settlement occurs when funds are exchanged between card issuer and card acquirer to finalize the transaction; at this stage, merchants receive payment, and cardholders are billed (Payfirma, 2016).

Case Study 4.4: Thales/Gemalto

Thales is a global technology leader known for its innovations in quantum applications, AI, 6G, and cybersecurity. Governments, institutions, and companies in the defense, aerospace, space, and digital identity sectors rely on Thales' products and services to carry out critical missions and make informed decisions (Thales, 2023). In early 2019, Thales acquired international security company Gemalto and combined it with its existing digital assets to create a global leader in digital security. As organizations around the world undergo digital transformation, they will benefit from the combined innovation of Thales and Gemalto (Thales, 2024a). Gemalto's activities have been integrated into Thales' Digital Identity and Security Division, further strengthening its cybersecurity offering.

Digital Identity and Security includes: (Thales, 2023)

- Banking and Payment Services
- Cloud Security and Identity and Access Management
- Identity and Biometrics
- Mobile User and Device Authentication
- Cybersecurity Solutions

Gemalto, a global leader in digital security, was at the forefront of the evolving digital landscape. As billions of people around the world seek secure ways to communicate, travel, shop, bank, entertain and work anytime, anywhere, Gemalto played a critical role in facilitating these experiences (Gemalto, 2014). Thales offers a wide range of products, including secure personal devices such as smart cards and tokens, as well as secure software and managed services—all essential to maintaining the integrity of digital interactions. In addition, Thales provides secure payment technologies, including the EMV smart cards used in banking, which are critical to ensuring secure financial transactions.

4.7 Payment Card Industry Data Security Standards

PCI DSS was developed to improve the security of payment account data and promote the global adoption of standardized security measures. It applies to all entities involved in payment processing, including those that store, process, or transmit cardholder data and sensitive authentication information. Cardholder data includes PAN, cardholder name, expiration date, and verification codes. Sensitive authentication data used to authenticate cardholders and authorize payment transactions includes, but is not limited to, card verification codes, full track data, PINs, and PIN Blocks (PCI SSC, 2024b).

The objectives and requirements of PCI DSS (PCI SSC, 2024b) are outlined below.

A. Build and Maintain a Secure Network and Systems

1. Install and maintain network security controls.
2. Apply secure configurations to all system components.

B. Protect Account Data

3. Protect stored account data.
4. Protect cardholder data with strong cryptography during transmission over open, public networks.

C. Maintain a Vulnerability Management Program

5. Protect all systems and networks from malicious software.
6. Develop and maintain secure systems and software.

D. Implement Strong Access Control Measures

7. Restrict access to system components and cardholder data by business need to know.
8. Identify users and authenticate access to system components.
9. Restrict physical access to cardholder data.

E. Regularly Monitor and Test Networks

10. Log and monitor all access to system components and cardholder data.
11. Test the security of systems and networks regularly.

Issuers	PSPs
Card Production	PIN Security
Logical	PIN Transaction Security Point of Interaction
Physical	PTS Hardware Security Module
Token Service Provider	Point-to-Point Encryption
PCI 3-D Secure Core	PCI 3-D Secure Software Development Kit
	Software-Based PIN Entry on COTS
	Secure Software
	Secure Software Lifecycle
	Contactless Payments on COTS
	Mobile Payments on COTS

Fig. 4.7 PCI Security Standards Ecosystem (PCI SSC, 2024a)

F. Maintain an Information Security Policy

12. Support information security with organizational policies and programs.

Figure 4.7 illustrates the PCI Security Standards from the perspectives of both issuers and PSPs.

PCI DSS requires four key steps to protect payment account data (PCI SSC, 2022):

- Assess: Identify where payment account data, inventory IT assets, and business processes related to payment processing. Analyze vulnerabilities, implement necessary controls, and undergo a formal PCI DSS assessment.
- Remediate: Address security gaps, remediate vulnerabilities, securely eliminate unnecessary data storage, and implement robust business processes.
- Report: Document the assessment and remediation steps, and then submit compliance reports to the accepting entity, typically an acquiring bank or payment brands.
- Monitor and Maintain: Ensure that security controls are consistently implemented, and that the environment operates effectively throughout year. These processes should be integrated into the organization's security strategy to ensure continuous protection.

4.8 Tokenization

Tokenization is a security technology that replaces sensitive card information with non-sensitive, randomly generated numeric sequences during transactions (Fiserv, 2025). This process ensures data integrity during storage, processing, and transmission. For card payments, tokenization replaces cardholder's PAN with a unique token that is securely transmitted for payment, while the original data is stored in a protected token vault.

Key features of tokens include:

- Each token is unique.
- Tokens are randomly generated.
- Tokens consist of numeric and alphanumeric strings.
- Token and the original data have no logical or mathematical relationship.
- Tokens are irreversible, meaning that original data cannot be retrieved.

Tokenization offers several benefits, including simplifying PCI DSS compliance by reducing the complexity and cost of managing sensitive payment card data. It improves user experience by enabling transactions without requiring users to re-enter their payment details, thereby reducing shopping cart abandonment rates. For card issuers, tokenization reduces operational costs by outsourcing token storage and original data management to the TSP. It also allows issuers to quickly adapt to technological advances and regulatory changes. By replacing card data with tokens, tokenization significantly improves payment security and reduces the risk of data breaches. It supports both single-use and reusable tokens to meet data privacy requirements. It ensures compliance with EMV Tokenization Specifications for both issuers and acquirers using EMV-compliant payment cards. In addition, tokenization streamlines integration with banks, card schemes, and PSPs by minimizing the need to transfer sensitive data between payment systems.

Token Service Provider

TSP is a company in payment ecosystem responsible for issuing and managing tokens, including mapping card numbers to payment tokens

(Fiserv, 2025). The company operating the Token Service Platform is FinTech.

TSPs generate unique tokens using cryptographic algorithms to ensure both security and uniqueness. They develop and provide tokenization APIs for banks and PSPs to enable seamless integration. To maintain security, TSPs build and operate infrastructure that ensures accurate mapping between tokens and original data while restricting access to sensitive information. They also oversee the entire token lifecycle, managing creation, distribution, monitoring, and revocation of tokens to ensure their validity and security. In some cases, TSPs facilitate clearing and settlement processes between banks and PSPs. In addition to enhancing security, TSPs help reduce operational costs for card issuers by simplifying the deployment and management of tokenization systems. By hiding sensitive information, they improve data privacy and reduce the risk of data breaches. In addition, TSPs support regulatory compliance for data storage and transmission while streamlining card processing. As a result, issuers can focus on their core business without compromising security or compliance.

Case Study 4.5: PCI SSC

PCI SSC is a global consortium dedicated to the development, enhancement, and implementation of security standards for the protection of payment account data. Its mission is to strengthen global payment security by establishing standards and providing services that promote education, awareness, and practical implementation among stakeholders. The consortium accomplishes this through a strategic framework that aligns its initiatives with its mission and addresses the needs of global payments industry (PCI SSC, 2024a).

Key Functions of PCI SSC:

- PCI SSC creates and maintains comprehensive security standards to safeguard card data and payment systems.
- PCI SSC regularly updates the standards to address evolving threats and new technologies.
- PCI SSC facilitates global adoption by providing training, certification programs, and resources to help organizations in achieving compliance.
- PCI SSC provides customized guidance to help organizations of all sizes meet their security requirements.

- PCI SSC conducts campaigns, workshops, and educational events to promote best practices in payment security.
- PCI SSC certifies and manages Qualified Security Assessors who conduct on-site security assessments to ensure compliance with PCI Standards.

CHAPTER 5

Digital Banking

Abstract This chapter explores the transition from traditional to digital banking, highlighting the growth of internet banking, web banking, and app banking. It examines the infrastructure of digital banking, focusing on user interface design, data security, and scalability. It also discusses the emergence of challenger banks and neobanks that use technology to deliver hyper-personalized services. Advanced technologies such as AI, ML, and DL are identified as key drivers of innovation and operational efficiency. The chapter concludes with an analysis of regulatory frameworks and financial sustainability models, positioning FinTech as a transformative force in reshaping the global economy.

Keywords Digital banking · App banking · Web banking · Challenger banks · Neobanks · API banking · BaaS · AI banking · Beta banks

Electronic banking refers to banking services delivered through electronic channels, including internet, mobile devices, ATMs, and telephones that allow users to conduct transactions remotely. This category includes both innovative digital banking solutions and the adaptation of traditional banking services to digital platforms (Alt & Huch, 2022).

T. Geçer and V. Akgiray, *The Financial Technology Revolution*,
https://doi.org/10.1007/978-3-031-92048-6_5

- Electronic Banking
    - Digital Banking
        - Internet Banking
            - Web Banking
            - App Banking
    - ATM Banking
    - Telephone Banking

Digital banking refers to services delivered through web and mobile platform applications and represents an evolution of traditional banking methods. It increases user satisfaction and loyalty by leveraging technological advances and promoting widespread adoption (Majumdar & Pujari, 2022). Accessible anytime and anywhere, and all at once, digital banking has emerged as a dominant alternative to traditional banking. Key benefits include secure and seamless access from any location, and the ability to support multiple users simultaneously. By integrating web services and mobile applications, digital banking offers a full range of services, including accounts, cards, loans, payments, investment services, and insurance. It allows users to conduct transactions independently, reducing reliance on physical branches and improving operational efficiency. In addition, digital banking personalizes services by analyzing user behavior and preferences, turning satisfaction into loyalty. By catering to tech-savvy users, it helps retain existing users and attract new ones, driving ongoing innovation in FinTech sector.

Key characteristics of digital banking can be summarized as follows:

- Technology: Digital banks invest heavily in back-office infrastructure to meet increasing regulatory requirements and to automate internal processes (Gasser et al., 2018). This infrastructure includes servers, databases, and networks designed to ensure both security and efficiency. They prefer cloud-based technologies, which allow for extensive data scalability and effective management.
- Cybersecurity: Protecting sensitive information is critical. Cybersecurity uses encryption, firewalls, and multiple layers of protection to prevent unauthorized access and data breaches.
- User Interface: Well-designed user interface is essential for the success of digital banking. UX/UI principles guide the development of web services and mobile applications, significantly improving overall user experience.

- Hyper-Personalization: Customizing user experience comprises personalized interactions that enhance user satisfaction and foster loyalty.
- Data Analytics and AI: Digital banks use data analytics to gain insight into user behavior, manage risk, and deliver personalized services. AI and ML enhance decision-making processes and improve operational efficiency.
- Regulatory Technology: Digital banking complies with increasingly strict AML and KYC regulations. These technologies facilitate rapid adaptation to evolving regulatory standards (Gasser et al., 2018).

Core Banking System

Core banking system is the spine of digital banking, providing a framework for managing, storing, and securing banking services. It must prioritize security, reliability, efficiency, scalability, and flexibility to ensure seamless performance. Frequent updates are essential to integrate new technologies and adapt to evolving user needs. The rise of API banking, open banking, challenger, and neobanks emphasize the need for more adaptable core banking systems. To remain competitive, traditional banks must embrace digitization and successfully transition to digital banks.

Core banking system has three layers:

Interaction Layer

Interaction layer serves as main user interface for the banking system. It includes essential components such as UX/UI design, mobile and web platforms, personalized services, customer support, security protocols, and system integration.

Application Layer

Application layer manages and secures banking operations through microservices, modules, and integrated systems. It ensures the scalability, reliability, security, and efficiency of core banking functions. Key components include APIs, protocols, frameworks, and operational modules. Unlike the interaction layer, application layer manages back-end operations, enabling service delivery.

Data Layer

Data layer stores, processes, and manages all banking information. It optimizes data retrieval and ensures the efficient and secure handling of large volumes of data while integrating with other layers to maintain operational integrity, continuity, and regulatory compliance.

5.1 Internet Banking

Internet banking allows users to access to banking services through web platforms and mobile applications on internet-connected devices. Internet banking versions are listed below.

- Web Banking 1: Banking services are offered through web browsers on fixed devices.
- Web Banking 2: Banking services are offered through web browsers on mobile devices.
- App Banking 1: Banking services are offered through applications on fixed devices.
- App Banking 2: Banking services are offered through applications on mobile devices.

Table 5.1 shows all possible versions of internet banking.

The success of internet banking depends on several key factors. User-friendly interface, with intuitive menus, buttons, and visuals, is essential for smooth navigation across web services and mobile applications. Robust security measures, including encryption, multi-factor authentication, and regular updates, are crucial for protecting user data. Convenient access allows users to engage with banking services anytime and anywhere, and all at once, ensuring consistent functionality across all devices. Smooth integration with core banking systems, card schemes, PSPs, and

Table 5.1 Internet Banking matrix

Internet banking	*Fixed devices*	*Mobile devices*
Web Banking	1	2
App Banking	3	4

third-party services facilitates effective synchronization. Advanced technologies such as APIs, AI, ML, and DL drive continuous innovation and improve operational efficiency. Personalization is vital, as tailored services based on user behavior, preferences, and habits enrich overall experience. The system must be scalable to accommodate increasing numbers of users and transaction volumes. Simplified transactions allow users to complete banking activities instantly on both fixed and mobile devices. Continuous updates introduce new features based on user feedback and market trends to meet evolving needs. In addition, 24/7 support provides real-time assistance with user issues.

App Banking

App banking assumes that smartphones are mobile computers with telephony capabilities that facilitate the delivery of comprehensive banking services. As a subset of digital banking, app banking has experienced rapid growth with the advancement of mobile technology. Its success can be attributed to its user-friendly interface, convenience, and intuitive design (Majumdar & Pujari, 2022). The primary value proposition of app banking is to provide anytime, anywhere, and all at once all accessibility through simple, mobile-optimized interfaces. Applications are easy to install and enable users to perform banking tasks without visiting a branch, ATM, or call center, thereby increasing convenience and usability. App banking platform supports a wide range of services, including account management, payment cards, loans, investments, payments, money transfers, and foreign exchange services. Customization features allow users to tailor the app to their specific needs, with real-time alerts to keep them informed of account activity, transactions, and security issues. Known for its efficiency and cost-effectiveness, app banking offers faster and more economical services compared to traditional banking forms.

Web Banking

Web banking allows users to access financial services through a web browser, providing a seamless and convenient online experience. It offers instant access to more complex services that allows users to manage their finances anytime and anywhere, while built-in security measures protect sensitive data. Key benefit of web banking is its cost-effectiveness, as it eliminates the need for physical branches, staff, and extensive infrastructure. Web banking also increases efficiency by quickly processing high transaction volumes and improving overall user experience. Web banking platforms deliver tailored services and increase engagement by analyzing user behavior and spending patterns. Continuous investment in technology attracts tech-savvy users, while value-added services generate additional revenue and improve overall bank performance.

Web Banking vs. App Banking

- Access Method: App banking works through mobile applications on smartphones or tablets, while web banking is accessible through web browsers on desktops, laptops, or mobile devices.
- Service Offerings: App banking primarily provides basic services, while web banking offers more complex banking solutions for both individual and corporate users.
- Additional Features: App banking excels in location-based services, while web banking offers a broader range of features.
- User Interface Design: App banking applications use streamlined layouts optimized for the smaller screens of mobile devices, while web banking offers more detailed interfaces designed for larger screens.
- Target Users: App banking primarily targets individuals, whereas web banking serves both individual and corporate users.
- Compatibility: App banking requires the development of separate applications for both Android and iOS operating systems, while web banking can be developed using programming languages designed specifically for web browsers.
- Corporate Preferences: Corporate users prefer web banking because it offers a more feature-rich and complex set of services that better meet the needs of corporations in managing advanced financial tasks.
    - Restricted User Group: Corporate users have restricted access to banking platforms to enhance security and protect sensitive financial data.
    - Authorization Procedures: Corporate users generally require additional approvals to ensure compliance with corporate policies.
    - Access Times and Locations: Corporate users tend to bank during business hours and from office locations.
    - Focus on Corporate Offerings: Banking services should prioritize features tailored to corporate users, including high-value

transactions, import–export operations, corporate lending, and treasury management.

Case Study 5.1: Nubank

Nubank is the most prominent digital bank outside of Asia, serving more than 105 million users in Brazil, Mexico, and Colombia. It has transformed the industry by leveraging data and proprietary technology to deliver innovative financial products and services. Guided by its mission to simplify financial services and empower people, Nubank promotes financial inclusion and advocates for responsible lending through transparency. Its efficient and scalable business model balances low operating costs with high growth returns and has been recognized with numerous awards (Nubank, 2024). Nubank offers diverse financial services branded as its "five financial seasons": spend, borrow, save, invest, and protect (Nubank, 2023). Its product portfolio includes credit cards, bank accounts, personal loans, insurance, investment accounts, and cryptocurrency services, positioning it as Latin America's leading financial SuperApp. As a comprehensive financial platform, Nubank is expanding its market presence through strategic partnerships, such as its collaboration with Uber. By continuously diversifying its services, Nubank is consolidating its role as a dominant player in digital finance (Rubini, 2024).

Nubank's Approach

- No-Fee Structure: Nubank's zero-fee policy eliminates traditional banking fees, making financial services more accessible to unbanked and underbanked.
- Digital-First Approach: By operating entirely online, Nubank avoids the overhead costs of physical branches, allowing lower fees and offering more competitive interest rates.
- User-Centric Design: platform prioritizes a seamless user experience by offering an intuitive mobile applications and streamlined account management tools.
- Revenue Streams: While many of Nubank's core products are offered for free, the bank generates revenue through loan interest, card transaction interchange fees, and its rewards program. In addition, Nubank diversifies its revenue by offering investment products and insurance services.

5.2 ATM Banking

ATMs are self-service, unmanned banking machines that provide access to essential financial services. These machines allow users to perform basic transactions such as cash withdrawals, deposits, and bill payments. Strategically located, ATMs provide both convenience and security, ensuring seamless access to banking services. ATM banking uses payment cards, QR codes, digital wallets, and mobile applications to enhance user experience. Key benefits of ATM banking include 24/7 availability, which reduces dependence on bank branches and enables bank staff to focus on more complex tasks. ATMs extend banking services beyond regular business hours, enabling fast and efficient transactions without long waiting times. In addition, ATM banking complements web and app banking, providing consistent experience across digital and physical platforms.

5.3 Telephone Banking

Telephone banking allows users to access banking services via a landline or mobile phone and conduct transactions through call centers or dedicated lines. Although less common due to the rise of digital banking alternatives, it is still valued for its accessibility, although some transactions may incur fees. Despite its decline, telephone banking offers significant advantages. It provides 24/7 access, allowing users to manage accounts, process payments, apply for loans, invest, transfer funds, and handle foreign exchange outside of standard banking hours. Key benefit is the direct, personalized assistance available; users can consult bank representatives for guidance. Security is a top priority, with robust authentication measures in place to protect transactions. Phone banking complements web and app banking, creating a multi-platform experience. It is especially important in emergencies, enabling urgent transactions such as money transfers and balance inquiries. It also serves as an alternative for users without internet access or with limited digital literacy, ensuring financial inclusion.

5.4 Challenger Banks

Challenger bank is a newly emerged retail bank from that disrupts traditional banking by offering a streamlined, digital-first approach rather than relying on physical branches (Alt & Huch, 2022). These banks challenge conventional financial institutions by integrating modern banking technology with innovative digital solutions to provide a more efficient, user-centric experience. Unlike traditional banks, which are often constrained by outdated infrastructure, challenger banks leverage AI, ML, and DL to deliver hyper-personalized financial services. Their value proposition is to increase competition and drive industry innovation through digital technologies. By customizing services to meet individual user needs, they significantly improve overall banking experience. Operating with lower overheads, challenger banks offer cost-effective and transparent pricing. They build trust through clear communication, simplified services, and straightforward fee structures. Challenger banks continuously improve their offerings, prioritizing user satisfaction and accessibility. They have a profound impact on the market, responding quickly to trends and updating their services accordingly. This adaptability forces traditional banks to innovate, fostering a more dynamic and competitive financial sector.

5.5 Neobanks

Neobanks are fully digital financial institutions that use technology, big data, and advanced analytics to deliver banking services primarily through smartphone applications and online platforms (BIS, 2024). As a next-generation financial model, neobanks offer hyper-personalized services exclusively through digital channels. They differentiate themselves from traditional banks by leveraging cloud computing, APIs, big data, and AI to ensure 24/7 access to banking services. Targeting millennials and Generation Z, especially users under the age of 30, including students, neobanks aim to foster long-term user loyalty. Primarily their appeal lies in seamless mobile access, offering transparent, low-cost services with easy-to-use experience. This digital-first approach is particularly beneficial to underbanked populations that traditional banks tend to overlook. Thus, neobanks often serve underbanked population (IMF, 2022).

Figure 5.1 illustrates the different types of neobanks, distinguishing between licensed and unlicensed forms and highlighting their roles as producers, wholesalers, and retailers in financial ecosystem.

Neobanks offer various financial products, including demand and time deposit accounts, feature-rich payment cards, customized lending

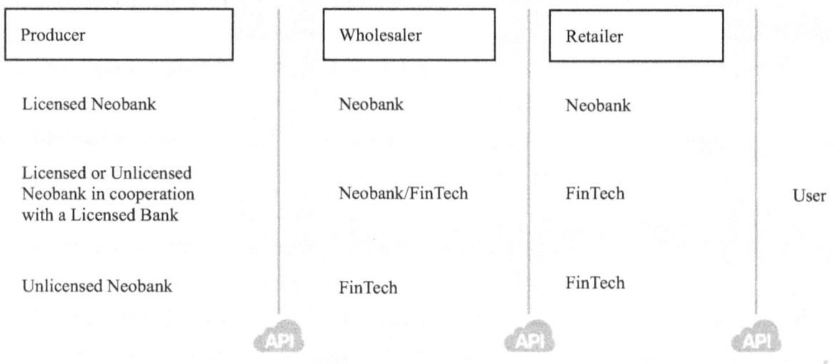

Fig. 5.1 Types of Neobanks

solutions, and investment options in stocks, bonds, derivatives, and cryptocurrencies. They also enable both domestic and international money transfers and offer convenient programmable payment services.

Neobanks can be divided into four versions based on their legal status:

- Version 1: Neobanks operate without a traditional banking license and may not be subject to banking regulations in some countries.
- Version 2: Neobanks have a full banking license and comply with all applicable banking regulations.
- Version 3: Neobanks operate under a limited banking license, which may exclude deposit insurance based on local regulations.
- Version 4: Neobanks may have either a full or limited banking license; but often choose to partner with a licensed traditional or digital bank. This collaboration allows them to offer banking services and deposit insurance through their partner bank.

Technically, a licensed neobank is as a bank, while an unlicensed neobank is FinTech.

Neobank Revenues

Neobanks generate revenues from a variety of sources, including fees and commissions related to credit and payment card transactions, payments, loyalty programs, and prepaid mobile phone top-ups. They also generate income from the marketing and distribution of financial products such as investments, insurance, and money transfer services. In addition, neobanks generate interest income from credit card balances, retail loans, deposits, government securities, and other interest-bearing instruments (Nubank, 2023). They can also generate transaction-based income, which includes interchange fees, ATM fees, cash deposit fees, inbound euro conversion fees, and money transfer fees (Monzo, 2024). In addition, neobanks earn income through API licensing, distribution, and partnerships with traditional banks, card schemes, and PSPs. These diverse revenue streams increase operational efficiency while enabling competitive service offerings.

Case Study 5.2: KakaoBank

Founded in 2017, KakaoBank was one of the first internet-only banks in South Korea, along with Kbank and Toss Bank. The rapid growth of mobile banking has been driven by BigTech companies like Kakao, reflecting a global shift in financial services (Kim et al., 2023). KakaoBank, a subsidiary of Kakao Corp., South Korea's leading mobile communications company, operates a diverse portfolio that includes messaging, e-commerce, payments, banking, ride-hailing, music streaming, and webtoons. Kakao generates revenue across multiple industries, including AI, healthcare, cloud computing, and venture capital investments. The company has also expanded into mobility, entertainment, and gaming (Kakao Corp., 2024).

KakaoBank has quickly become a leader in South Korean banking industry by offering competitive rates, seamless services, and innovative features. It appeals to a diverse user base, ranging from tech-savvy millennials to traditional users seeking modern banking solutions. By competing with both traditional and digital banks, KakaoBank has accelerated the adoption of digital banking in South Korea and had a significant impact on the broader financial sector. Primarily mobile-focused, KakaoBank offers a wide range of services through its easy-to-use applications. Its intuitive interface reflects the bank's commitment to digital innovation, improving accessibility and user experience.

Core Services

By leveraging AI and data analytics, KakaoBank offers personalized financial advice, improves fraud detection, and provides responsive customer support, further solidifying its leadership in digital banking. The bank also offers personal loans—such as unsecured, home, and credit loans—through a streamlined digital application process. In addition, KakaoBank issues credit cards that seamlessly integrate with its digital ecosystem and facilitates easy domestic and international money transfers through its money transfer application.

5.6 API Banking

API banking uses APIs to integrate digital services in the financial sector, enabling impeccable data transfer between core banking systems and external services (Alt & Huch, 2022). This technology enhances user experience and improves banking efficiency. API banking can be implemented in three different ways.

Open API Banking

Public (open) APIs connect PSPs, banks, and third-parties, providing data access based on open standards (BIS, 2022). These APIs increase transparency, support open banking regulations, and promote growth, scalability, and interoperability. They enable PSPs to offer payment initiation and account information services to banks through APIs, thereby expanding banking services and improving accessibility.

Figure 5.2 illustrates the structure of API banking by mapping public, partner, and private APIs for third-parties, partners, app banking, and web banking.

Partner API Banking

Partner APIs enable API banks to connect to partner banking systems and deliver personalized services through dedicated APIs. These APIs are accessible to pre-defined users, typically from partner organizations (BIS, 2022). This collaboration allows API banks to integrate with other banks, PSPs, card schemes, and technology companies, thereby expanding service offerings and improving interoperability.

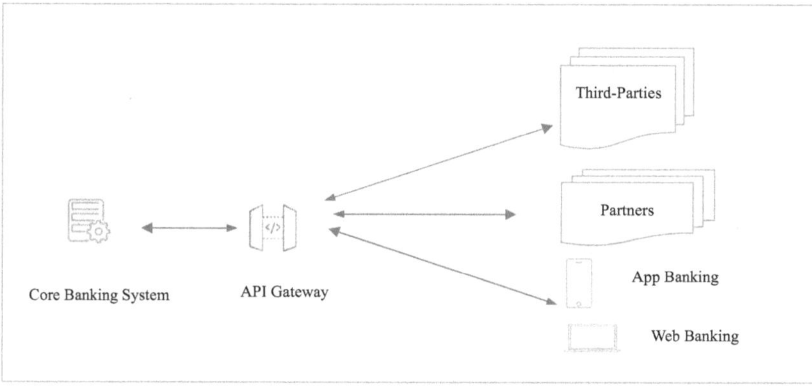

Fig. 5.2 API Banking

Internal API Banking

Private (internal) APIs facilitate the secure transfer of data in a bank's internal systems. They are designed for authorized personnel and ensure seamless integration between core banking system, web services, and mobile applications (BIS, 2019a).

Advantages of APIs

APIs are revolutionizing banking industry by improving collaboration, scalability, performance, security, and compliance (Nordic APIs, 2018). They enable banks to innovate, analyze user data, improve user experience, and reduce development costs, thereby providing a competitive advantage. In addition, APIs give banks greater control over their financial data, ensuring both security and compliance with global standards. By facilitating secure integration with third-party applications, APIs generate valuable insights, foster innovation, and create new banking opportunities. APIs also streamline transactions by providing immediate responses to user requests, increasing efficiency and user satisfaction.

API Banking Revenues

API banks offer various subscription models for access to their services, with fees based on usage time, capacity, or specific features. They can also implement a pay-per-use model, charging fees for each API request. In addition, API banks generate revenue through revenue-sharing agreements with PSPs. The data exchanged between API banks and PSPs can be monetized, with each API call incurring a fee set by API bank.

Case Study 5.3: Tinkoff

Tinkoff is a Russian FinTech company known for its innovative and comprehensive approaches. Initially launched as a direct-to-user credit card provider, Tinkoff's fully online model set it apart from Russia's traditional branch-based banking system. Over time, the company expanded its offerings beyond credit cards to include a broader range of financial services. In 2013, Tinkoff rebranded as Tinkoff Bank to reflect its evolution into a digital-first bank.

Tinkoff's mission is to provide a comprehensive range of financial services, simplifying banking while increasing accessibility and efficiency. The bank aims to be an all-encompassing financial platform, leveraging technology and innovation to deliver high-quality services without the need for physical branches. As a fully online bank, Tinkoff offers a wide range of financial products, ranging from traditional banking services to investment solutions. Its focus on innovation and digital technology enables it to provide seamless and efficient services, catering to Russia's increasingly tech-savvy population (Rubini, 2024). Through its mobile app and web interface, Tinkoff's ecosystem offers individuals and corporates an extensive selection of financial and lifestyle services. At its core is Tinkoff Bank, one of the largest online banks in the world, serving over 40 million users (Tinkoff, 2024). To drive growth, Tinkoff took advantage of key opportunities in financial market (Bavrova, 2021).

- Tinkoff has reduced its dependence on credit card cycles by diversifying its range of financial products and services.
- It introduced new non-credit revenue streams, including corporate, SME, and retail banking accounts, as well as wealth management, corporate payroll processing, and merchant services.

Tinkoff has developed a comprehensive financial ecosystem aimed at increasing its share of users' wallets by integrating related services and products.

5.7 Open Banking

Open banking enables banks to securely share user-authorized data with third-party developers and providers, facilitating the creation of innovative applications and services (BIS, 2019a). This model is transforming the way users access financial products through the use of APIs provided by financial institutions (Nordic APIs, 2018). As the foundation of open banking, APIs facilitate secure, automated communication between systems from different companies with the consent of users (Hensen & Kötting, 2022). The primary goal of open banking is to encourage innovation, competition, and collaboration in the financial sector. Operating in a regulatory framework cultivates a dynamic ecosystem where third-parties, such as PSPs, can integrate with the banking sector.

This integration enhances financial services and expands access to underbanked and unbanked population, thereby promoting financial inclusion. Open banking has stimulated disruptive business models, particularly by increasing financial transparency and accessibility (Deloitte, 2021a). It facilitates data sharing and allows third-parties to initiate payments directly from users' accounts, providing an alternative to traditional credit and debit card transactions. Open banking also allows financial institutions to share product information and service-level metrics, such as user satisfaction scores (Reynolds, 2017). The EU's PSD2 requires banks to share account information and payment initiation services. Account information services allow users to view and manage their accounts and payment cards from a single platform. Payment initiation services allow users to make payments and transfers through a single platform. While these services offer significant benefits, the debate continues as to whether they provide enough value to drive widespread adoption of open banking.

Advantages of Open Banking

Open banking offers several important benefits. It stimulates market growth by encouraging new entrants, banks, and PSPs to deliver more competitive products and services. It also facilitates the secure exchange of information, thereby enhancing data protection and privacy. Through open banking, financial tools such as aggregation, analysis, monitoring, recommendations, automation, and payment requests improve and streamline money management (Reynolds, 2017). Key advantage of open banking is its capacity for innovation, as it fosters the development of new financial products tailored to evolving user needs. It also creates new revenue streams for banks and PSPs through API access and data sharing, which supports comprehensive data analysis and reporting in open banking ecosystem. Security remains a top priority, with open banking ensuring robust risk management while complying with regulations such as the EU's PSD2 and other regional laws. Finally, open banking promotes collaboration, encouraging banks and PSPs to partner, expand the market, and drive continuous innovation.

Open Banking vs. API Banking

- Scope: API banking uses private, public, and partner APIs, while open banking relies primarily on public and partner APIs.
- Standardization: Open banking requires the implementation of standardized APIs, while API banking can use either customized or standardized APIs depending on the agreements.
- Legal Obligation: Open banking is legally mandated to provide services such as account information and payment initiation, while API banking operates on the basis of mutual agreements without regulatory requirements.
- Purpose: Open banking promotes collaboration with third-parties to drive financial innovation, while API banking focuses on collaboration between banks and their partners.
- Security: Open banking relies on a robust infrastructure to protect sensitive data, especially account information and payment initiation. In contrast, API banking requires a more comprehensive security framework that includes both internal and external systems.

5.8 Banking as a Service

BaaS is a business model that allows FinTech companies and other third-parties that meet a bank's security, legal, and compliance standards, to integrate banking products into their offerings without the need to obtain banking licenses. This model allows third-parties to leverage a bank's regulatory infrastructure (Feyen et al., 2023). BaaS provides a comprehensive solution that ensures the seamless execution of banking services (Schueffel, 2017). Through BaaS, non-banks can offer banking services such as accounts, payment cards, loans, payments, and investments through APIs. This approach enhances their value proposition by allowing them to provide banking services directly to their users. The company operating the BaaS Platform is FinTech.

Figure 5.3 illustrates the transformation of core banking modules into financial services in BaaS model, highlighting key components such as accounts, payment cards, loans, payments, and foreign exchange modules.

Advantages of BaaS Model

BaaS model offers several advantages that enable non-banks to quickly deliver modular and customized financial products through market-facing APIs. This model simplifies integration and offers a wide range of services, ensuring a seamless experience for both users and providers

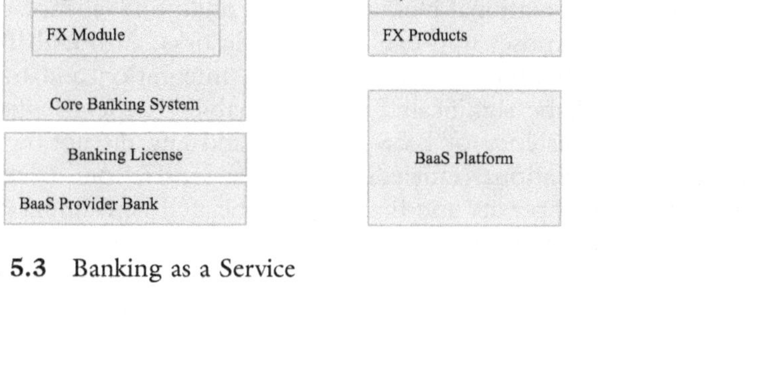

Fig. 5.3 Banking as a Service

(Deloitte, 2021b). By leveraging BaaS infrastructure, non-banks can efficiently develop innovative financial products—such as account opening and lending services—without incurring the significant costs associated with maintaining core banking systems. This integration allows non-banks to leverage the risk management and compliance services of licensed banks, thereby enhancing their product offerings and expanding their user base.

BaaS improves cost efficiency by scaling operations, specializing services, and commoditizing financial products. It integrates these services into platforms with large user bases, encouraging the development of financial solutions tailored to real-world needs (Gcinisizwe et al., 2022). In addition, BaaS facilitates rapid prototyping and testing, enabling institutions to quickly launch new products, reinterpret traditional banking services, and integrate with the broader banking ecosystem through API-driven data exchange.

Disadvantages of BaaS Model

BaaS model presents several challenges for non-banks. Major drawback is the high cost and resource burden associated with complying with ever-evolving local and global regulations, which can be particularly challenging for smaller players. In addition, non-banks often have limited control over the infrastructure and services provided by BaaS platforms, limiting their ability to customize offerings, meet user expectations and fully optimize their value proposition. Privacy and data protection are critical concerns, especially when sensitive financial and non-financial user data is shared between providers and users. While sharing personal data enables unbanked to access financial products, it also poses significant security and compliance risks (Gcinisizwe et al., 2022). Integration challenges may arise between the non-bank's IT infrastructure and BaaS platform, leading to operational inefficiencies. In addition, reliance on a single BaaS provider exposes non-banks to specific risks. Although BaaS reduces the cost of obtaining a banking license, integration and maintenance costs can still be significant. Service reliability depends on the performance and consistency of BaaS provider, and any disruption can negatively impact operational efficiency and user satisfaction. Furthermore, the technical complexity and high costs associated with integrating multiple APIs from different parties present additional challenges to BaaS model.

Case Study 5.4: Solarisbank
Based in Berlin, Germany, Solarisbank AG is a FinTech company specializing in BaaS solutions that enable banks and non-banks to offer financial services without the need for a banking license. By providing simple and efficient banking solutions, Solarisbank enables businesses to seamlessly integrate financial services into their core offerings (Gcinisizwe et al., 2022). Operating on a platform-based model, Solarisbank provides banking services through APIs, enabling non-banks—including FinTech companies, e-commerce platforms and technology companies—to integrate financial products into their user experience. Solarisbank generates revenue from service, licensing, and transaction-based fees, positioning itself as a key enabler in European banking industry.

Business Model of Solarisbank

Solaris provides a secure and robust infrastructure that enables partners to integrate compliant financial services into their offerings. All products are developed and maintained on a production platform accessible via APIs, ensuring seamless digital integration. The company primarily targets EU and UK markets, with a strong focus on Germany. Key target groups include large corporations, national and international banks, as well as technology and e-commerce companies with large user bases. In addition, FinTech companies remain a core segment for its business (Solarisbank, 2023).

Solarisbank Services (Solarisbank, 2024).

- Digital Banking Services
- Digital Assets and Crypto
- Lending Services
- Compliance and Security Solutions
- KYC Platform
- Savings and Investment Services

5.9 AI Banking

Infectious AI technologies are transforming banking industry and accelerating the transition to digital and AI-powered banking. This transition is redefining banking landscape and its value proposition. AI banking represents an evolution toward fully autonomous, unmanned banking. Four key trends highlight the growing demand for AI banks: rising user expectations driven by the widespread adoption of digital banking, increased utilization of advanced AI by leading financial institutions, disintermediation of traditional services by digital ecosystems, and the expansion of technology giants into financial services as part of their broader business strategies (McKinsey, 2024a).

AI banks offer several advanced capabilities, including:

- User Services: AI-powered robots and virtual assistants manage requests, assist with transactions, provide real-time services, and offer personalized recommendations to enhance user experience.
- Security: AI banks use data analytics to identify operational and transactional anomalies, supported by a real-time monitoring framework designed to address vulnerabilities.
- Credit Scoring: AI algorithms analyze both quantitative and qualitative data to improve the accuracy and efficiency of credit scoring.
- Regulatory Compliance: AI banks use AI-driven monitoring and reporting systems to ensure compliance with regulations such as AML and data security standards.
- Algorithmic Trading: AI algorithms analyze market trends, optimize portfolios, and refine trading strategies to improve financial performance.
- Customized Recommendations: AI banks provide hyper-personalized financial advice by analyzing user behavior, spending patterns, and risk tolerance.
- Process Automation: AI banks automate document processing and information management, thereby reducing operational costs and increasing productivity.
- NLP: AI banks use NLP to interpret queries, provide instant assistance, and analyze text data to improve interactions and decision-making.

AI Banking Revenues

AI banks generate revenue through multiple channels. They charge subscription fees for access to their services and earn transaction fees from payment cards and POS services. Significant portion of their revenue comes from interest income, as AI algorithms optimize loan portfolios to maximize returns. In addition, AI banks offer wealth management services, charging management fees for AI-driven financial solutions. Another important revenue stream is the monetization of anonymized user data for market research while ensuring compliance with privacy regulations. AI banks also capitalize on up-selling and cross-selling by promoting new or enhanced financial products to existing users. They also generate revenue through strategic partnerships based on revenue-sharing agreements and by licensing AI algorithms to other companies for financial decision-making and risk management.

5.9.1 Beta Banks

New banking models continue to emerge in response to ever-changing user preferences, expectations, demands, and technological advances. One of these newborn models is the "beta bank," which differs from traditional banking structures by emphasizing continuous innovation and operating as a platform-based service under the license of a parent bank, known as an "alpha bank." Unlike traditional banks, beta banks do not have a banking license; instead, they operate in the regulatory framework and branding of their parent bank. Beta banks are designed to be more compact, agile, innovative, and streamlined, with efficient workflows, targeted user bases, and advanced IT architectures with specific risk profiles.

They prioritize flexible pricing strategies and a user-centric approach to increase operational efficiency and improve overall user experience. While maintaining a distinct identity, beta banks remain closely aligned with their alpha bank, facilitating collaboration and resource sharing. Technically, a beta bank is FinTech.

Strategies for Differentiating Beta Banks from Alpha Banks

Beta banks differ from their parent banks in several key ways. As a controlled environment for testing new products, technologies, and business models, they develop innovative solutions that differ from traditional banking services. This approach allows beta banks to target niche markets, including unbanked and underbanked, emerging markets, and FinTech companies, by offering tailored financial services that address specific needs. Key differentiator is their user-centric approach, which allows them to deliver highly personalized services that set them apart from traditional banks. With a greater appetite for risk, beta banks explore unconventional business opportunities that can generate higher returns while taking greater risks. They streamline operations and drive continuous innovation by integrating AI, ML, DL, and data analytics. Their agile structures enable them to adapt quickly to market changes and technological advances. By enhancing web and app banking platforms with cutting-edge technologies, beta banks create services that differentiate them from traditional banks. This strategy builds brand awareness and expands their user base without the immediate need for a banking license. Once they have established strong market penetration, beta banks can apply for a banking license to further expand their service offerings.

Beta Bank Revenues

Beta banks generate revenue through a variety of channels, including subscription fees, account management fees, payment cards, loans, and investments. They also earn income by facilitating payment services, processing money transfers, and offering insurance products. Interest in personal loans is another important source of income. Beta banks also benefit from card processing, POS services, and brokerage commissions on financial products. The introduction of programmable payment options, budgeting tools and tax management solutions has further driven revenue growth. Beta banks operate in a broader financial ecosystem, engaging in BaaS, BNPL, embedded finance, and third-party revenue-sharing agreements. These diverse revenue streams enable beta banks to expand their offerings and increase profitability.

CHAPTER 6

Novelties in FinTech

Abstract This chapter explores key FinTech innovations, beginning with BNPL, which allows users to divide payments into installments, making high-value purchases more accessible and boosting sales. Another significant innovation is embedded finance, which integrates financial services into non-financial platforms, allowing merchants to offer accounts, payments, cards, loans, and investments in their products-thereby increasing convenience and promoting financial inclusion. SuperApps consolidate multiple services, such as payments, e-commerce, and entertainment, into a single platform, enhancing user engagement through a seamless experience. Neobrokers, which are digital-first trading platforms, attract younger investors by offering lower fees, fractional shares, and innovative revenue models such as payment-for-order-flow. RTO financing allows users to rent goods with the option to purchase, while EMI plans provide predictable financing for large purchases through fixed monthly payments. A2A payments facilitate direct bank transfers, bypassing card schemes, reducing merchant transaction fees, and offering a more efficient payment alternative.

Keywords BNPL · Embedded Finance · SuperApps · Neobrokers · RTO · EMI · A2A

T. Geçer and V. Akgiray, *The Financial Technology Revolution*,
https://doi.org/10.1007/978-3-031-92048-6_6

6.1 BNPL

BNPL allows users to purchase goods without paying the full price upfront and then pay the balance in interest-free installments (Accenture, 2021). This flexible payment solution is widely available on e-commerce platforms, online marketplaces, and retail stores. The increasing popularity of BNPL is driven by evolving user behavior, growing demand for alternative payment methods, and the expansion of digital payment options. With the advancement of FinTech, banks and financial institutions have integrated BNPL into their service offerings. In addition, QR codes, mobile payments, and digital wallets have simplified transactions, further increasing the appeal of BNPL. Initially gaining traction in e-commerce, BNPL has since expanded into various sectors. Examples include "Fly Now, Pay Later" for airlines, "Travel Now, Pay Later" for travel companies, and "Educate Now, Pay Later" for educational institutions, all of which have seen notable success. Industries using BNPL have reported significant growth and improved financial performance. However, rising inflation and interest rates threaten the sustainability of BNPL model (Worldpay, 2023). The company operating the BNPL Platform is FinTech.

BNPL Methods

Pay by Installment

Pay by Installment is a payment plan that allows users to divide their purchases into manageable installments, making high-value transactions more affordable. This model typically refers to split payment options such as interest-free pay-in-3 or pay-in-4 plans (Paypers, 2023). BNPL provides instant and flexible financing for a wide range of products and services through digital wallets, credit cards and payment accounts, including electronics, appliances, education, healthcare, furniture, and luxury goods. Merchants benefit from increased sales and user acquisition by making large purchases more accessible. In addition, this model enhances user experience and drives revenue growth, creating value for both users and merchants.

Pay Later

Pay Later is a payment option that allows users to defer purchases to a later date. This model represents a significant revenue opportunity for e-commerce platforms, online retailers, and merchants. The growing adoption of BNPL across multiple shopping channels is enhancing merchants' ability to leverage technology, improve user experience and drive user loyalty, making it an essential element of modern payment ecosystems.

Pay on Finance

Pay on Finance allows users to spread the cost of large purchases over time through either interest-bearing or interest-free payments, depending on the terms. Promotional interest-free installments on select products increase affordability and simplify checkout process. For merchants, this model increases sales of premium products by offering a flexible payment option. Predictable installment payments contribute to stable cash flow and financial security. In an inflationary environment, long-term payment plans—especially those with low or no interest—help users manage financial burdens and make large purchases more accessible. Ultimately, this model increases financial flexibility and stability for both users and merchants.

Finance Providers in BNPL

BNPL Platform

BNPL platform operates as a lender, allowing users to postpone payments while effectively managing credit risk. This model enables platform to offer comprehensive financing solutions to merchants, facilitating rapid scalability and fostering strategic partnerships with banks and card schemes. By streamlining the shopping and payment processes, BNPL enhances user experience while optimizing payment collection for merchants. This smooth integration not only improves user experience but also increases sales and strengthens platform's relationship with its merchant partners, driving mutual success.

Merchants

Some merchants self-fund BNPL model by taking on credit risk in a competitive market. Rather than requiring upfront payment, this approach allows users to defer payment after purchase, providing greater flexibility for specific products or brands in BNPL ecosystem. However, merchants must rigorously assess users' creditworthiness and actively manage receivables to mitigate risk. Robust credit policies are essential, as defaults can result in collection costs and legal fees associated with recovering overdue payments. Effective risk management and thorough user evaluation are critical for merchants who self-fund BNPL.

Card Schemes

By integrating with BNPL model, card schemes can expand their reach and increase card usage, ultimately increasing merchant acceptance. This strategy improves accessibility, increases card usage, and adds value to payment services. Integrating BNPL platform simplifies and expedites transactions, strengthening the role of card schemes in global payments ecosystem. In addition, by assuming financial responsibility and credit risk, card schemes enable BNPL platforms and merchants to focus on their core business, ensuring a seamless and efficient checkout experience.

Banks

As major players in financial system, banks have extensive expertise in credit risk management. They facilitate installment payments through payment cards, loans, and direct debits. Under BNPL model, banks can leverage their risk assessment capabilities to improve financial stability and ensure safer, more sustainable operations for both users and merchants. By overseeing financial management and conducting credit assessments, banks mitigate risk and improve transaction efficiency in BNPL.

Advantages for Users

BNPL platform improves the payment experience by streamlining checkout process and allowing users to pay in installments with a single click. This feature eliminates the need to repeatedly enter payment data and eases the financial burden by spreading costs over time rather than requiring a full upfront payment. With low-interest or no-interest plans, BNPL options provide a cost-effective alternative to traditional loans or credit cards, offering flexible monthly or weekly payment schedules to fit users' budgets. BNPL providers often subsidize or waive the costs associated with short-term credit by charging merchants a fee, thereby reshaping users' credit models (Tijssen & Garner, 2021).

Key benefit of BNPL is its accessibility to users without credit cards (cardless BNPL), those with limited credit histories, or those who prefer not to use traditional credit cards. It increases purchasing power by facilitating installment payments for high-value items, while prioritizing user experience, fostering user loyalty, and strengthening brand perception. Platform provides instant approvals by quickly assessing users' creditworthiness and allowing them to select customized installment plans at checkout. In addition, BNPL platforms often offer promotions and discounts on selected products or during special events to increase user value. Payments can be made through various digital channels, including web services, mobile applications, bank accounts, digital wallets, and payment cards. These platforms serve as alternative financing solutions that extend credit access to unbanked population. Consistent, on-time BNPL payments can also improve credit scores, allowing users to qualify for better credit terms in the future.

Disadvantages for Users

BNPL can lead users to accumulate debt beyond their financial capacity (Sifted, 2022). BNPL model, particularly with long-term installment plans, can result in high interest charges, putting users in financial jeopardy and increasing the risk of repayment difficulties. Missed payments can result in additional interest, late fees, and potential legal consequences, exacerbating debt problems and limiting users' financial options. In addition, late or missed payments can adversely affect credit scores, reducing the chances of obtaining future loans or credit. BNPL platforms often impose strict credit limits based on a user's financial history, which can leave some users unsatisfied and unable to access needed funds. In addition, some platforms require a credit check and approval for each purchase, making the process time-consuming and inconvenient. The short-term repayment plans typically offered by BNPL providers may not be suitable for users seeking longer-term financing solutions.

Advantages for Merchants

BNPL products increase sales by providing a seamless and transparent financing solution that offers greater flexibility than traditional payment methods (Visa, 2022). BNPL reduces shopping cart abandonment by allowing users who do not have immediate funds or have reached their credit card limits to complete their purchases. Merchants benefit from BNPL by earning interest on financed purchases, promoting premium products, and increasing average order values. BNPL increases revenue by increasing basket size, encouraging repeat purchases, attracting new users, improving checkout conversion rates, and strengthening brand positioning (Accenture, 2021). BNPL providers invest heavily in advertising and marketing to drive user demand, while merchants use co-branded marketing to highlight the availability of BNPL at checkout (Tijssen & Garner, 2021). In addition, targeted marketing, advertising, and search engine optimization increase merchant visibility and facilitate product discovery for users.

From a financial perspective, BNPL services help stabilize cash flow and mitigate the risk of unpaid receivables. Depending on the agreement, credit risk can be managed by BNPL platform, a bank, or a card scheme, simplifying the collection process for merchants. BNPL platforms comply with international standards, ensuring secure transactions, efficient dispute resolution and reduced legal costs. In addition, BNPL provides valuable insights into user behavior, spending patterns and payment histories, enabling merchants to optimize inventory and pricing strategies. By streamlining collections and offering multiple payment options, BNPL increases financial stability, accelerates revenue growth, and improves overall business performance.

Advantages for Banks

BNPL model enables banks to offer innovative lending solutions, enhancing user satisfaction and loyalty through flexible and convenient financing options. Banks are well-positioned to introduce cutting-edge payment solutions, leveraging emerging models such as BNPL to strengthen their value proposition (McKinsey, 2021). This approach results in increased payment card usage, higher transaction volumes, and overall user spending, ultimately leading to greater bank revenues. By appealing to younger demographics, BNPL helps banks attract new users while retaining existing ones. Additionally, BNPL allows banks to introduce new lending products and diversify their loan portfolios. By spreading credit risk across multiple stakeholders, banks can manage risk more effectively and reduce exposure to non-performing loans. Collaboration among banks, BNPL platforms, card schemes, and merchants expands user base and enhances revenue. Merchants benefit from accepting business cards, while banks provide the necessary payment infrastructure and POS services. This synergistic partnership drives financial growth and strengthens the broader financial ecosystem.

Advantages for Card Schemes

Credit card schemes can offer BNPL services to all partner merchants (Sifted, 2022). BNPL model allows card schemes to increase transaction volume, generate additional revenue and expand their user base, particularly by providing financing options to users with poor credit or younger demographics. This is especially important for millennial and Generation Z users, who tend to prefer BNPL and often lack strong financial relationships with traditional banks (Visa, 2022). By partnering with BNPL platforms, merchants and banks, card schemes can establish revenue-sharing agreements that improve economic performance. This model also fosters user loyalty through flexible payment options, while providing precious insights into spending habits that can be used for targeted marketing strategies. In addition, BNPL simplifies international transactions, allowing users to make cross-border purchases while enabling card schemes to generate foreign exchange revenue from currency conversions. This approach supports global expansion by helping card schemes reach new merchants and users in different countries through BNPL platforms. By facilitating these transactions, BNPL increases brand visibility for card schemes, providing a competitive advantage and differentiation in the marketplace.

BNPL Platform Revenues

BNPL platforms generate revenue through various channels, including merchant fees, interchange fees, interest income, and service fees (Affirm, 2023). Their primary source of revenue is merchant discount rate, which consists of a percentage of sales plus a fixed transaction fee (Sezzle, 2023). Additional sources of revenue include pay-per-use fees for transactions such as credit card processing, loans, and money transfers. BNPL platforms also monetize value-added services through up-selling and cross-selling to both users and merchants. In addition, subscription-based revenues represent another significant revenue stream (Sezzle, 2023). They earn interest in funds and charge penalties for late payments. Foreign exchange fees are generated, especially for cross-border transactions. Servicing revenue is generated from contractual fees charged to third-party loan holders and unconsolidated securitizations that BNPL platforms earn by managing loan portfolios (Affirm, 2023).

Case Study 6.1: Klarna

Founded in 2005 in Stockholm, Sweden, Klarna initially specialized in online payment solutions using BNPL model, which offers deferred payment options (Yan, 2023). The company's vision is to redefine shopping and payments by prioritizing user-centric solutions and delivering innovative, hyper-personalized financial services. With approximately 150 million global users and 2.5 million daily transactions, Klarna operates an AI-powered platform designed to enhance the shopping experience through fairness, sustainability, and convenience (Klarna Holding, 2023). Klarna also allows users to shop and pay in installments without the need for a credit card (KoreFusion, 2021).

How Does Klarna Work? (Stripe, 2024a)

To use Klarna, users should select it as their preferred payment method during checkout on e-commerce websites, mobile applications, or in physical stores. They can manage their Klarna accounts through Klarna app, which enables them to track orders, view payment plans, make payments, and access customer support. Klarna offers three main payment options.

- Pay in 4: Split purchase into four equal, interest-free installments. The first payment is due at checkout, and the remaining three payments will be made over the following six weeks.
- Pay in 30: Pay the full amount within 30 days without incurring any interest or fees, as long as the payment is made on time.
- Long-Term Financing: This refers to financing options for larger purchases that involve extended credit terms that are subject to interest rates and approval.

Klarna's Value Proposition to Merchants

Klarna partners with more than 550,000 retailers worldwide, engaging users throughout the shopping journey to drive growth and provide an alternative to global marketplaces. The company connects retailers with users through content creation partnerships, dynamic search advertising and virtual shopping experiences. Klarna supports retailers by reducing their working capital needs through secure payment solutions and credit products for both e-commerce and physical stores. Its comprehensive services include advertising and marketing to increase merchant visibility, technology-driven credit risk management for secure transactions, user insights and analytics to improve user targeting, and integrated user services for priceless support. With its smooth integration, global reach, and compatible checkout experience, Klarna ensures that merchants receive upfront payments while assuming the credit risk for both users and merchants (Klarna Holding, 2023).

6.2 Embedded Finance

Embedded finance is the seamless integration of financial products into non-financial platforms (Feyen et al., 2023). This approach allows non-financial companies to integrate financial services into their offerings, processes, or products, thereby increasing both the value of platform and the lifetime value of its users (Ozili, 2022).

Today, companies in a variety of industries—such as retail, healthcare, education, and tourism—are integrating financial services, including accounts, payment cards, and insurance. For example, merchants are enabling seamless in-app transactions to increase convenience and user loyalty. The primary appeal of embedded finance lies in its ability to enable non-financial companies to offer banking and payment services directly to users (KoreFusion, 2021). The value of embedded finance extends beyond individual financial services, positioning it as a transformative force in financial innovation. Embedded financial services are primarily used for high-value transactions (Visa, 2023b). The company operating the Embedded Finance Platform is FinTech.

Figure 6.1 ironically illustrates the concept of embedded finance, highlighting that its value proposition is greater than the sum of finance and product value propositions.

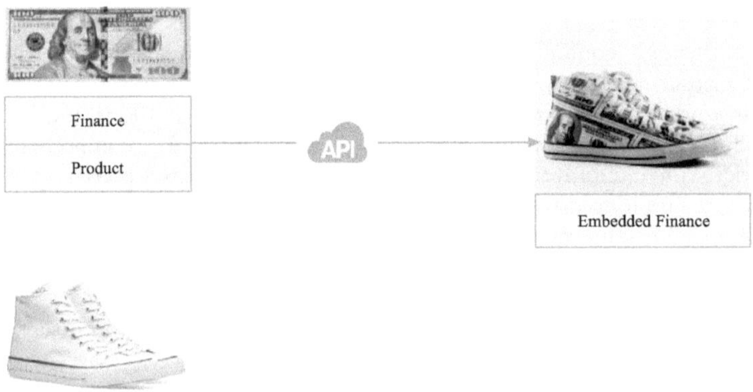

Fig. 6.1 Embedded Finance

Types of Embedded Finance

Embedded Accounts

Non-financial companies now offer embedded account services that allows users to open and manage accounts directly through web services or mobile applications. This integration improves user experience by facilitating seamless financial transactions in a merchant's platform, thereby simplifying processes for both users and businesses (McKinsey, 2022).

Embedded Cards

Non-financial companies partner with banks, card schemes, and PSPs to issue payment cards, improving user experience and streamlining transactions for both users and merchants.

Embedded Loans

Non-financial companies offer embedded credit services that allow users to access financing options at checkout. This model enhances purchasing flexibility, facilitates installment plans, and increases sales by making high-value products more accessible.

Embedded Payments

Non-financial companies are increasingly integrating payment services into their platforms, including mobile payments, money transfers, digital wallets, and QR code payments. These solutions are becoming more deeply embedded in merchant ecosystems (Visa, 2023b).

Embedded Investment

Non-financial companies are increasingly integrating investment services to provide users with seamless access to stocks, derivatives, cryptocurrencies, funds, and other financial instruments. This integration increases accessibility, improves portfolio management, and fosters greater engagement with money and capital markets.

Embedded Insurance

Non-financial companies partner with banks and insurance providers to integrate a variety of insurance services, including property and casualty, health, life, and retirement plans.

Figure 6.2 illustrates the transformation of financial products as they transition from financial institutions to non-financial companies through embedded finance platforms. These platforms facilitate offerings such as embedded accounts, cards, loans, payments, investments, and insurance.

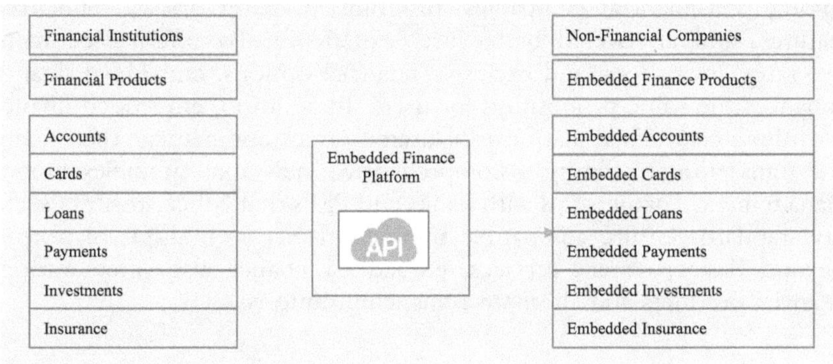

Fig. 6.2 Types of Embedded Finance

Embedded Finance vs. BaaS

While embedded finance and BaaS are related concepts, they differ in scope and application.

- Embedded finance integrates financial services into non-financial platforms, allowing users to access payments, credit, and insurance as part of their daily activities. This model enhances user experience by making financial services seamless and readily available in non-financial ecosystems.
- BaaS refers to licensed banks that make their banking infrastructure available to FinTech companies, PSPs, and other third-parties. This model allows these companies to offer banking services—such as account management and payment processing—without having to obtain their own banking licenses. While embedded finance focuses on enhancing user experience by integrating financial services into non-financial platforms, BaaS serves as the back-end infrastructure that supports FinTech companies' financial offerings.

Advantages for Users

Embedded finance delivers significant benefits to users by integrating financial services into shopping platforms. This integration allows users to manage their purchases and finances without having to switch between applications or platforms. It encourages competition and innovation among non-financial companies, resulting in better pricing, enhanced features, and an overall better user experience. By offering competitive rates, lower fees, and exclusive financial options, embedded finance enhances the value proposition for users. In addition, embedded finance provides a centralized platform for users to track and manage their financial transactions, offering a comprehensive view that simplifies money management. Partnerships with banks and PSPs that adhere to strict security standards ensure compatible transactions across multiple platforms. Beyond basic payment services, embedded finance also offers various financial products and alternative financing options.

Advantages for Merchants

For merchants, embedded finance creates new revenue streams, expands market reach, generates recurring revenue, reduces user acquisition costs, improves unit economics, and minimizes friction at checkout (Dealroom.co, 2022). By embedding financial services, platforms can increase average revenue per user and improve user retention with minimal additional acquisition costs (Harris et al., 2022). Embedded finance increases revenue and profitability by integrating financial services into merchant ecosystem. It improves the payment experience by reducing checkout abandonment and simplifying transactions. Automated accounting and financial management increases operational efficiency, allowing merchants to streamline their accounting processes. In addition, embedded finance enables any business to offer financial services, opening up new opportunities for growth (Ozili, 2022). Embedded finance enables merchants to use user data to provide personalized financial solutions. By analyzing user behavior and preferences, merchants can tailor their offerings to individual needs, thereby increasing user satisfaction. The integration of financial products fosters user loyalty, as users value the convenience of accessing financial services in familiar platforms, reducing their dependence on external providers. In addition, platforms can cross-subsidize costs by providing POS software and hardware, using payment revenue to offset hardware costs, ultimately reducing overall costs for merchants (Harris et al., 2022).

Advantages for Banks

For banks, embedded finance expands their user base and market share while increasing user loyalty. By leveraging new distribution channels, banks can deliver faster and more accessible banking products, thereby increasing user engagement and satisfaction. This model provides banks with valuable data from non-financial platforms, offering business intelligence insights into user behavior, preferences, and financial needs. Banks can use this data to refine their products and develop targeted marketing strategies, resulting in more personalized and effective financial services. The rise of embedded finance is driven by evolving user expectations and an emphasis on supply-side economics for banks (Visa, 2023b). This model enables banks to enrich their revenue streams through transaction fees, payment processing, lending, and other financial services. Similar to open banking, embedded finance benefits all stakeholders by fostering partnerships between banks and non-banks, creating seamless financial solutions in everyday platforms (Hensen & Kötting, 2022).

Embedded finance plays a critical role in promoting financial inclusion by offering banking services to underbanked and unbanked population with limited access to traditional financial services. Non-financial platforms, such as e-commerce websites, integrate financial products like payment accounts and credit options to bridge the gap for users excluded from the banking system. This strategy enhances user lifetime value by increasing revenue per user while minimizing acquisition costs, ultimately contributing to a more inclusive and accessible financial ecosystem.

Embedded Finance Platform Revenues

Embedded financial platforms generate revenue through various channels, including subscription fees from users, merchants, and third-parties. They may charge fees for financial transactions, such as payments, lending, or investment services, and earn interest on loans originated through their platform. In addition, these platforms receive commissions from affiliated merchants for the sale of goods or services, creating another revenue stream. Referral fees based on insurance premiums for embedded insurance products also contribute to their overall revenue.

Case Study 6.2: Apple Embedded Finance

With the launch of the Apple Card, Apple is further expanding into embedded finance by leveraging its large user base and ecosystem to provide impeccable financial experience. By integrating financial services directly into its platform, Apple enhances user convenience, strengthens user loyalty, and increases engagement (Boboev, 2024). WhiteSight (2023) identifies three distinct phases in Apple's financial evolution, highlighting its growing influence in the economic landscape.

Embedded Finance 1.0: A Crush

Initially, Apple relied on telecom carriers and financial institutions for device financing, while third-party insurers provided protection services.

Embedded Finance 2.0: It is complicated

From 2014 to 2019, Apple strategically acquired patents and partnered with financial institutions and technology providers to launch key products, including Apple Pay and Apple Card.

Embedded Finance 3.0: Commitment

Since 2020, Apple has shifted from relying on external partnerships to developing its own financial infrastructure. The company has acquired U.S. payment and lending licenses, improved its payment processing and fraud detection tools, and used data to refine its financial products and expand its ecosystem. Apple's embedded financial strategy has positioned the company as a formidable player in FinTech sector, competing with both conventional banks and emerging technology companies. By leveraging its large global user base and seamlessly integrated ecosystem, Apple is challenging financial institutions with offerings such as Apple Pay, Apple Card, and Apple Wallet. In near future, Apple may broaden its financial services to include banking, insurance, and investments.

6.3 SuperApps

SuperApp is an operating system that supports multiple applications on a single platform, ultimately turning user satisfaction into loyalty. WeChat, which originated in the Far West and launched in 2012, has pioneered this model, evolving from a messaging app into a comprehensive SuperApp that offers food delivery, e-commerce, financial services, and entertainment. In addition to stand-alone financial services, WeChat also serves as an integrated payment system, facilitating seamless transactions. SuperApp strategy encourages diversification and enables companies to enter new markets with innovative products. The company operating the SuperApp Platform is FinTech.

SuperApps Approaches

Single or Multi-Developer Approach

In single-developer approach, FinTech company develops the entire SuperApp platform, starting with its core business and gradually adding related services. In contrast, multi-developer approach integrates third-party applications while preserving its core business, with SuperApp acting as an aggregator. This strategy leverages external innovation, allowing SuperApps to expand their offerings through collaboration and improve overall ecosystem.

Top-Down or Bottom-Up Approach

The top-down approach establishes core SuperApp framework and integrates additional services to create a unified platform. In contrast, bottom-up approach prioritizes the development of core business and architecture first and then adds complementary applications as platform evolves. This approach ensures a robust foundation before introducing new features and services.

Thematic or General Approach

Thematic approach focuses on a specific industry and integrates core and complementary applications to provide specialized services. In contrast, general approach spans multiple industries and integrates a variety of commercial applications to create a comprehensive, multi-service platform.

Design of SuperApps Platforms

Platform provides a secure and convenient payment infrastructure that integrates multiple products and services into a unified system. Its architecture ensures seamless compatibility with multiple service providers, simplifying API connections and data management. With security as a top priority, platform is regularly updated to protect users' financial data from unauthorized access. Its intuitive and customizable interface facilitates easy navigation, while a modular structure optimizes administration, testing, and feature updates. Designed for scalability, platform efficiently handles high traffic and large user volumes without compromising performance. Analysis of user data personalizes the experience and creates a dynamic, visually appealing interface. Continuous improvements based on user feedback increase customization and overall satisfaction.

Features of SuperApps Platforms

Single Platform

SuperApps serve as a unified platform, eliminating multiple stand-alone applications (Fasnacht, 2021). They integrate services across content, design, and access, ensuring seamless interactions between different applications. Single sign-on system eliminates the need for multiple usernames and passwords. This integrated structure simplifies data sharing and allows users to efficiently manage their information in a single account, improving usability and overall user experience.

Unified Payment Application

SuperApps provide a frictionless payment experience through a single application that integrates multiple payment methods, including bank accounts and payment cards. This integration simplifies transactions by eliminating to switch between payment options at checkout.

Core and Complementary Businesses

Each SuperApp has a core function that was established in its early years; over time, additional features have been integrated into platform (Ye, 2023). This core application serves as the primary value proposition and facilitates the seamless expansion of services. For example, WeChat began as a messaging and social networking app before evolving to include payment, and entertainment services.

Multiple Applications

SuperApps unify core business functions, payment systems, and additional services on a single platform, enhancing user experience and streamlining access to multiple functions.

Figure 6.3 outlines the business structure of SuperApps, categorizing its operations into core, complementary, and supplementary segments.

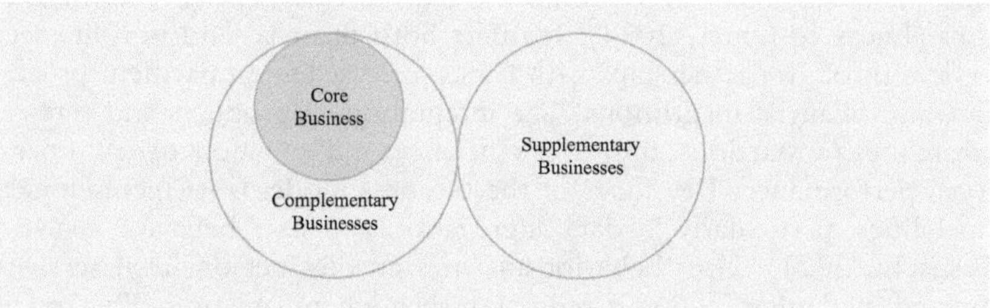

Fig. 6.3 Businesses in SuperApps

Advantages for Users

Platform integrates multiple applications into a seamless digital ecosystem that effectively meets user needs in a cohesive environment. Users experience services in a fluid, contextual, integrated, and centralized manner (Lucas & Lopes, 2024). An easy-to-use interface improves navigation and minimizes learning curve. Streamlined payment system reduces login and processing times, improving overall efficiency. Platform analyzes shopping and transaction data to deliver hyper-personalized user offerings, In addition, a robust framework ensures secure and consistent use of bank accounts, payment systems and cards.

Disadvantages for Users

SuperApps require users to share sensitive personal and financial information, including location and payment details, raising significant privacy concerns. Dependence on a single platform can limit user choice, while excessive market dominance can stifle competition and encourage monopolistic practices. Wide range of features can overwhelm users, and mandatory application installations can lead to storage and performance problems. In addition, overloading platform with too many services risks diluting its core value, potentially confusing users, and reducing its overall effectiveness.

Advantages of Platform

By making these applications available to users, SuperApp platforms aim to hyper-personalize their value proposition by collecting user data, which enables them to customize offers and marketing communications (Lucas & Lopes, 2024). It offers both financial and non-financial services through partnerships with banks, card schemes, payment processors, and financial institutions. The integration of products and services streamlines transactions, improves efficiency, and enhances overall operational performance. Key focus of the business model is its technological capabilities, particularly in data aggregation and user behavior analytics (Fasnacht, 2021). User behavior analytics enables personalized services, targeted marketing, and cost reduction through automation. This model improves user retention by centralizing essential services and minimizing reliance on multiple applications. Consistent design, functionality and feature sets support competitive pricing, while service engagement drives revenue. Secure and efficient payment processes enhance user experience, and enriched service offerings create opportunities for up-selling and cross-selling, further driving growth.

Disadvantages of Platform

Customizing interfaces for users, merchants, developers, and partners creates operational complexity and management challenges. Integrating multiple services into a single platform can dilute core offerings and drive users to seek specialized alternatives. Cluttered interface with too many applications can hinder navigation and reduce intuitiveness. Extending functionality and adding new features incurs significant development and deployment costs. Meanwhile, successful implementation requires highly skilled teams to develop and integrate new features into platform (Hasselwander, 2024). Wide range of services can overshadow core products, requiring additional effort to maintain visibility. Regulatory compliance across multiple services further complicates operations and increases costs. In addition, offering multiple applications can reduce platform uniqueness and limit personalized user experiences. Managing large volumes of data requires significant investment in robust security measures to protect user information. Another contentious issue is unfair competition, as SuperApps may gain an unfair advantage over smaller competitors, potentially disrupting market dynamics (Ye, 2023).

SuperApps Platform Revenues

Platform generates revenue through multiple channels, including subscription fees for premium features such as ad-free experience. It earns a percentage of revenue from in-platform and in-app purchases, including digital items, games, betting, and e-sports. Advertising revenues are generated from ads displayed on platform and in applications, with revenues depending on the type, duration, and content of ads. Collaborations with third-party service providers and developers further enhance revenues, particularly when their offerings align with platform's core services. Platform charges users for payment transactions and earns commissions by providing POS services to merchants. Additional revenue is generated from integrated payment cards and digital wallets. Platform can also monetize user shopping and payment data by reporting business intelligence insights to third-parties. Partnerships with banks, card schemes and PSPs enhance financial capabilities and expand revenue potential. These multiple revenue streams contribute to financial stability and long-term growth.

Case Study 6.3: Gojek

Gojek is Southeast Asia's leading on-demand platform, empowering micro-entrepreneurs, and improving urban accessibility. Inspired by Indonesia's informal motorcycle taxi (ojek) economy, Gojek launched in 2010 as a call center connecting users with drivers. It has since evolved into a multi-service platform offering mobility, food delivery, logistics, and more. With over 2.6 million driver-partners across Indonesia, Vietnam, and Singapore, Gojek is improving urban mobility and supporting local merchants (GoTo, 2024). The company's success is driven by its ability to address the region's public transportation challenges (Azzuhri, 2018).

Using a multi-sided platform model, Gojek connects users, service providers, and businesses, leveraging network effects to drive rapid growth. Key component of its strategy is GoPay, a digital payment service that facilitates transactions and supports Indonesia's large unbanked population. By integrating food delivery, bill payment, and money transfer into a single app, Gojek strengthens user engagement and retention. The company differentiates itself by consolidating multiple services into one seamless platform. Over time, it has evolved into a SuperApp, offering ride-hailing, food and package delivery, digital payments, logistics, lifestyle services, healthcare, entertainment, transportation, and business solutions. This expansion strengthens its competitive edge and expands its user base.

GoTo merger between Gojek and Tokopedia enhances Gojek's ability to compete with regional and global technology companies by expanding its platform and service offerings. Gojek's transformation from a ride-hailing startup to a leading SuperApp highlights its adaptability, leveraging technology and innovation to meet evolving user needs and capitalize on new market opportunities in a rapidly growing digital economy.

6.4 Neobrokers

Neobrokers are reshaping the investment landscape by attracting new investors, particularly from Generation Z. These platforms provide intuitive web services and mobile applications, increase financial inclusion, and encourage collaborative investing. By expanding access to equity markets, they encourage greater participation in the global economy

(Janussek, 2022). Their primary appeal lies in low-cost or commission-free brokerage services that democratize investment opportunities. By integrating with banks, card schemes and exchanges through APIs, they ensure secure and efficient transactions for financial instruments. The company operating the Neobroker Platform is FinTech.

Advantages of Neobroker Platforms

Neobrokers are adopting an all-digital strategy, offering brokerage services exclusively online to improve investor experience. Mobile applications streamline account registration, portfolio management and trading, allowing users to manage their investments in real-time. With significantly lower commissions and fees compared to traditional brokerages, neobrokers make investing more accessible. Fractional share trading and low minimum deposit requirements further expand accessibility, allowing users with limited capital to invest in high-priced stocks. These platforms offer access to multiple asset classes, including cryptocurrencies and global markets, helping users build diversified portfolios.

Users benefit from market data and financial news, enabling them to make more informed investment decisions. Many neobrokers also offer robo-advisory services and algorithmic trading tools to enhance portfolio management. By merging technology and finance, these platforms broaden access to investing, while integrations with budgeting tools help users monitor and optimize their financial health. Institutional investors benefit from API integrations that enable customized trading strategies for advanced portfolio management. Neobrokers also promote financial education and collaboration through social features such as interactive chat rooms and social trading forums where experienced investors share insights. By offering tailored products for unbanked and underbanked population, as well as automated savings plans, neobrokers actively promote financial inclusion.

Disadvantages of Neobroker Platforms

Neobrokers face several limitations, including a narrow selection of investment instruments and limited access to global markets due to regional regulations and currency restrictions. Compared to traditional brokerage firms, they may offer fewer research tools, limited market analysis and less comprehensive insight, making it difficult for investors who rely on these resources to make informed decisions. Customer support is often less robust, particularly for complex financial instruments, with fewer advisors available to provide personalized guidance. In addition, returns on idle funds in neobroker accounts may not keep pace with inflation or alternative investment opportunities. As mobile-first platforms, neobrokers may lack visual depth, advanced functionality, and analytical tools available on traditional web-based trading platforms. Newer entrants are more susceptible to regulatory changes and require ongoing compliance efforts to maintain investor confidence. Neobroker apps often incorporate gamified features and simplified interfaces to attract young investors and encourage active participation in the stock market. However, this approach can lead to risky, impulsive trading behavior (Janussek, 2022). The emphasis on short-term trading can increase transaction frequency, commission payments, and investment risks. Some platforms restrict trading activity by suspending buying or selling orders for certain assets, preventing users from executing trades at their desired price levels. This can undermine user confidence and raise transparency concerns. In addition, neobrokers may inadvertently steer inexperienced users toward speculative investments, exposing them to greater financial risk. Finally, concerns about payment-for-order-flow models and reliance on single trading venues (market makers) have led regulators to re-evaluate these brokers' practices (Meyer et al., 2021).

Neobroker Platform Revenues

Neobrokers generate revenue through multiple channels, with a significant portion of their revenue coming from payment-for-order-flow. This model allows them to offer lower user fees compared to traditional brokers, which rely primarily on transaction fees and commissions (Meyer et al., 2021). Transaction-based revenue is generated by routing user orders for options, cryptocurrencies, and stocks to market makers (Robinhood, 2024). In addition, neobrokers earn interest on margin loans collateralized by marketable securities, investments, and foreign government bonds. Other income comes from securities lending, where securities are lent to institutional investors for short selling. Bank deposits and cash balances in negative-yielding currency accounts also serve as sources of revenue (InteractiveBrokers, 2024). Neobrokers monetize market data by selling historical and real-time market information to traders and financial institutions. Foreign exchange transactions, particularly currency conversions in cross-border trading, contribute to their profitability. They also generate brokerage fees by providing retail investors with access to IPOs. Corporate transactions, including mergers, acquisitions, and dividend processing services, further enhance their revenue streams. These diverse revenue streams allow new brokers to maintain a low-cost business model while remaining profitable.

Case Study 6.4: Robinhood

Founded in March 2015, Robinhood revolutionized digital trading in U.S. by introducing commission-free stock and ETF trading through its mobile app. This innovation disrupted the traditional brokerage industry and made investing more accessible, especially for younger, tech-savvy investors. In response to high fees charged by conventional brokers, Robinhood eliminated trading commissions, significantly lowering barrier to entry. Platform has since expanded its offerings to include cryptocurrency trading, further diversifying its financial services (Columbia Engineering, 2024). By democratizing investing, Robinhood has driven the growth of retail trading and broadened market participation. Its commitment to accessible financial services continues to reshape the investment landscape, especially for younger generations.

Robinhood's Products and Services (Robinhood, 2023)

- Brokerage
- Investing
- Options Trading
- Fractional Trading
- Recurring Investments
- Robinhood Crypto
- Robinhood Wallet
- Robinhood Gold
- Robinhood Credit Card

Robinhood generates revenue primarily through payment-for-order-flow, in which it receives compensation from market makers for routing users' trades. While this model allows for commission-free trading, it has been criticized for potential conflicts of interest, raising concerns about whether trades are executed in users' best interests. Despite the regulatory scrutiny, Robinhood remains a major player in FinTech sector and continues to expand its offerings to meet evolving market demands.

6.5 Rent to Own

RTO is a retail business model that allows users to acquire household goods by making small, periodic payments (Anderson & Jackson, 2004). By combining the flexibility of renting with the benefits of ownership, RTO allows users to make incremental payments and eventually own the goods without having to pay the full price upfront (Guajardo, 2019). Initially popularized by retailers in Western economies for furniture and electronics, RTO has since expanded to various sectors, including software, vehicles, equipment, and real estate. The company operating the RTO Platform is FinTech.

RTO platforms serve unbanked and underbanked population who lack access to traditional credit for high-value purchases. These platforms allow users to try products before committing to ownership, effectively bridging the gap between renting and buying. Banks and PSPs recognize RTO as an innovative financing solution, driven by user demand for frequent upgrades and changing preferences. Merchants benefit by differentiating themselves in a competitive marketplace while offering users greater purchasing flexibility.

RTO model operates under a lease agreement that outlines terms, payment schedules, and a buyout option. Users make periodic lease payments and have the option to purchase the item at a premium, similar to a call option. This call option can be exercised at any time during lease term (American-style option) or only at the end of lease term (European-style option). Contracts specify a predetermined purchase price, and lessor typically covers maintenance, repairs, warranties, and insurance throughout lease term. This flexibility makes RTO an attractive financing alternative for both users and dealers.

Advantages of RTO Model

RTO model benefits low-income and financially disadvantaged individuals who do not have access to traditional credit. Users can compare financing options, access customer support, receive financial advice, and purchase insurance for both rented and owned items. The model provides access to premium products and the flexibility to rent before buying, making it particularly valuable for those with limited financial resources. RTO externalizes the cost of maintaining goods for users (Floyd, 2023). Users can immediately acquire basic items such as appliances, furniture, and electronics without having to pay upfront. In addition, the model may include a no-penalty option. At the end of the rental period, users can purchase the item by paying a fixed portion of the remaining rental fees or by securing an installment plan at a competitive rate (Anderson & Jackson, 2004). Fixed pricing models enhances cost transparency, helping users understand their total cost of ownership—an important feature in an inflationary environment. This model particularly benefits the unbanked, underbanked and those with low or unstable incomes, contributing to its popularity in developing markets. In addition to affordability, RTO allows users to experience or text products—such as household goods or real estate—before committing purchase. Rental payments typically contribute to the final purchase price, facilitating the gradual acquisition of ownership. In some cases, users can rent a portion of an asset while retaining partial ownership, providing access without requiring a full upfront payment.

The flexibility of the model reduces the pressure for immediate purchase commitments while encouraging timely payments to maintain the purchase option, minimizing the risk of missed payments. Many RTO platforms offer refinancing options for users who wish to purchase the asset, further increasing flexibility. Some platforms even allow for subleasing, creating rental arbitrage opportunities. Often, the asset itself serves as collateral, reducing the need for additional collateral when seeking credit. This combination of accessibility, ownership and financial flexibility makes RTO an attractive alternative for users seeking manageable financing solutions.

Disadvantages of RTO Model

RTO model can be more expensive than a traditional purchase due to accumulated lease payments and potential interest. The primary disadvantage of RTO is that it is an expensive form of financing. However, RTO is not classified as a loan, which means it does not incur traditional interest charges (Floyd, 2024). Ownership is not guaranteed until user exercises the call option, and the transition from lessee to owner can involve legal and financial complexities. Missed payments can result in repossession or forfeiture of the purchase option, adding to the financial burden.

In an inflationary economy, the final purchase price can be uncertain due to fluctuations in lease payments or product costs. While RTO works well for durable goods, it is less applicable to services or consumable products. Users should also be aware that initial deposits may not be refundable if they decide not to proceed with the purchase. High-value assets, such as vehicles or real estate, may require extended financing and leasing commitments. In addition, premiums paid for the call option are generally not refundable if user decides not to proceed. These factors should be carefully evaluated, especially for long-term or high-value commitments under RTO model.

RTO Platform Revenues

RTO platform generates revenue from several sources. It charges subscription fees to both users and merchants, and it earns commissions on rental and purchase transactions. RTO platforms should generate substantial rental revenue before items are sold and replacement costs are incurred, which requires a balance between rental and purchase revenue (Armaghan et al., 2023). In addition, offering insurance services for rented or purchased assets further increases income. Revenue-sharing partnerships with financial institutions, banks, card schemes and PSPs contribute to overall revenue. Platform generates business intelligence insights and reports by analyzing user data related to shopping, rental, and purchase behavior, and earns referral fees for directing users to banks or financial institutions. When acting as a product seller, rental income becomes a primary revenue stream. Platform also earns interest on loans and charges a premium for call options. It also generates additional revenue from product sales when users purchase rented items. Revenues from insurance, warranty, maintenance, and repair services further diversify and enrich the revenue streams.

6.6 EMI

EMI allows users to purchase goods and repay the cost in fixed monthly installments over a period of time. Initially adopted by traditional banks for high-value purchases such as real estate, vehicles, and electronics, EMI requires borrowers to make regular payments that cover both interest and principal, ensuring that the loan is fully repaid by the end of the term (Hasan, 2016). With the rise of digital banking, EMI has gained popularity due to its flexible repayment structure. EMI platform is as a marketplace that connects users with lenders, including merchants, banks, and card schemes. Unlike BNPLs, which offer short-term repayment plans, EMI typically offers extended repayment periods ranging from several months to several years, making it ideal for financing tangible goods, real estate, and high-value items. The company operating the EMI Platform is FinTech.

EMI payments are calculated based on the principal amount, loan term and interest rate set by the lender. Annuity formula, which considers the compounding of interest, determines payment structure. Installments can be scheduled monthly, quarterly, semi-annually, or annually. However, as frequency of installments increases, gap between the nominal and effective interest rates decreases (Hasan, 2016). Conversely, longer intervals typically result in higher effective interest rates due to the effects of compounding.

Types of EMI

Cardless EMI

Cardless EMI is an innovative payment method that allows users to access credit directly from banks or PSPs without the need for a traditional payment card. This method assesses creditworthiness based on a user's non-financial data (Malik et al., 2018), eliminating the need for financial data. This approach benefits users without payment cards, those making large purchases that exceed card limits (e.g., real estate or vehicles), and users who prefer not to use their cards for such transactions. By offering greater flexibility and accessibility, cardless EMI provides a convenient alternative to traditional card-based systems.

Card EMI

Card EMI allows cardholders to split their purchases into affordable installments, providing a secure and flexible financing solution. This option is particularly popular with users who prefer card-based transactions because it maintains the protections and benefits associated with payment cards while enhancing security.

Advantages for Users

EMI model makes large purchases more manageable by spreading payments over several months, thereby increasing financial stability. By dividing the cost into installments, users can budget effectively and avoid unexpected financial burdens. Platform simplifies the loan application process, expanding access to credit for unbanked and underbanked. Users can compare competitive loan offers from banks and PSPs, securing favorable rates and terms. Platform streamlines online loan applications, credit score monitoring, and loan management, eliminating the need for physical visits to banks. With fast approvals and instant fund transfers, EMI caters to users in need of quick financial assistance. Flexible repayment terms allow users to customize plans based on their financial capacity, helping them build credit scores and improve creditworthiness through consistent payments. In addition, cardless EMI options extend access to users without traditional payment cards, further promoting financial inclusion.

Disadvantages for Users

EMI platform has several disadvantages for users. Interest charges—whether fixed or variable—can significantly increase the total cost of the loan, especially over longer repayment periods. Early repayment penalties may apply, adding to the financial burden. Fixed payment schedule may not be suitable for users with irregular incomes, making repayment more difficult. In addition to interest, users may encounter hidden fees associated with loan applications, credit scoring, and other financial services. There is a risk of over-indebtedness if users accumulate more debt than they can manage. With fixed-rate loans, borrowers may end up paying more if interest rates fall, while variable-rate loans expose them to higher payments if interest rates rise, creating financial uncertainty.

Advantages for Lenders

EMI platform enables lenders to expand their user base and enrich their loan portfolios, reaching international users while streamlining multi-currency payment processing and collections. Automating the loan disbursement process reduces operational costs and improves workflow efficiency. Lenders receive real-time loan monitoring reports, enabling them to effectively monitor repayments. Platform encourages timely payments, reducing default risk and improving cash flow forecasting and liquidity management. It also provides POS services to merchants, creating new revenue streams. Data-driven algorithms improve credit scoring, enabling more accurate lending decisions. Platform's digital tools improve user engagement and loyalty by simplifying lending process.

EMI Platform Revenues

EMI platform generates revenue through multiple channels. Funds received from users are allocated in the following order: principal, interest, penalty interest and fees (Axis Bank, 2023). Platform earns subscription fees from both users and lenders, as well as interest income from direct financing of purchases. Early repayments may incur penalty fees, while missed EMI payments often result in late fees. Other revenue streams include processing fees for loan applications, approvals, documentations, disbursements, and collections. Insurance premiums on products also contribute to income. Platform benefits from currency parities and generates revenue from currency conversions for international transactions. It also monetizes analytical reports and payment data derived from loan processes. Additional revenue is generated through up-selling and cross-selling of financial products, including personal loans, digital wallets, payment cards, investments, and insurance. Advertising fees are charged for the promotion of products from banks, card schemes and PSPs. Platform may also earn commissions on loans originated by lenders and referral fees for directing users to e-commerce platforms, banks, investment firms, and insurance providers.

6.7 A2A

A2A payments are digital transactions that occur directly between accounts, bypassing traditional card schemes (Worldpay, 2023). While remittances have existed across markets for years, key innovation driving A2A adoption is the speed and ease of integration facilitated by open banking APIs and real-time payments (Juniper, 2023). These advances have accelerated adoption, making A2A payments faster and more cost-effective than card-based transactions.

A2A payments enable seamless transfers, including deposits, remittances, and direct payments. The primary benefit of A2A payments is the elimination of payment cards, which allows merchants to avoid fees such as merchant discount rate and reduce POS expenses. By excluding intermediaries, A2A payments improve cost efficiency and streamline transactions for both merchants and users. A2A payments are highly versatile, supporting a wide range of use cases, including subscription fees, utility bills, salaries, rent, credit, and card payments. They also facilitate complex transactions such as purchase payments, vendor settlements, money transfers, and investment trading, making them scalable and flexible solutions for various financial needs. In addition, A2A payments support all directions of money transfer, including M2M, P2P, P2B, P2G, B2G, B2B, and B2P. The company operating the A2A Platform is FinTech.

Figure 6.4 illustrates A2A payment flow, showing how transactions bypass traditional card schemes by connecting user's bank directly to merchant's bank through an A2A platform.

Advantages of A2A

A2A payments are integrated with open banking platforms to enhance payment initiation and account information services. This integration enables banks and PSPs, including those offering investment and insurance products, to incorporate A2A payments into their systems. By expanding access to unbanked and underbanked population, A2A payments promote financial inclusion and broaden market reach. With robust security measures, A2A protect sensitive data and ensure secure, fraud-resistant transactions. Unlike traditional bank or card-based systems, payments are processed instantly through digital channels, allowing merchants to receive funds without delay. However, A2A payments can introduce compatible at checkout by requiring users to enter their banking credentials and can present challenges in dispute resolution processes (McKinsey, 2024b).

A2A payments simplify international transactions by reducing currency conversion fees and enabling seamless global payments. Automation increases functionality by streamlining recurring and programmable

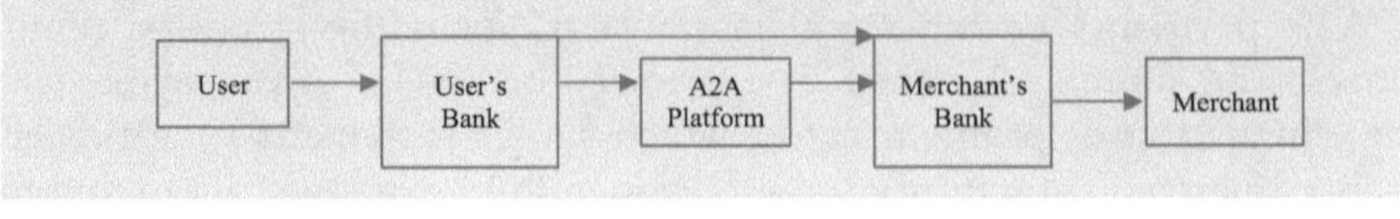

Fig. 6.4 A2A Flow

payments. A2A payments are widely used for bill payments and e-commerce and may eventually extend to POS systems. This transition highlights not only the cost-saving benefits of A2A payments, but also the challenges financial institutions must overcome to provide viable alternatives to debit and credit cards (McKinsey, 2024b). By bypassing traditional POS systems, merchants can eliminate processing fees and realize significant cost savings. In addition, digital data increases visibility, allowing merchants to efficiently track and reconcile payments, improving overall financial management.

Disadvantages of A2A

While A2A platforms offer convenience, they may lack the advanced security features typically found in traditional card schemes. Fraud prevention and error resolution can be more complex, making it difficult to reverse or cancel transactions. In addition, A2A platforms often impose transaction and daily limits, and users may incur higher fees for instant or cross-border transfers. Access to A2A services depends on merchant acceptance and technology infrastructure, which can be limited, particularly in rural areas. Not all merchants accept A2A payments, which restricts interoperability, especially in card-dominated markets. Because A2A interoperability requires collaboration among multi parties, successful implementation requires effective organization, leadership, and governance (Clark & Camner, 2014).

International transactions present additional challenges, including the complexity of currency conversions, different banking protocols, and global compliance requirements. Inconsistencies in A2A platform applications and procedures can confuse users and complicate transactions. The lack of globally accepted rules complicates chargebacks and dispute resolution, potentially causing delays or preventing problem resolution. In addition, the lack of a clear regulatory framework puts banks at a competitive disadvantage in establishing a robust presence in A2A payments market (McKinsey, 2024b).

A2A Platform Revenues

A2A platforms generate revenue through a variety of channels. They charge subscription and transaction fees for payments and money transfers, as well as additional fees for currency conversion for international transactions. Platform may also earn interest by investing user account balances in money market. Merchants using platform may be subject to API integration or licensing fees. Time between initiation of a payment and settlement of the funds generates additional yields. Users may incur fees for overdrafts or insufficient funds, while lending services generate additional interest income. Partnerships with banks, card schemes and financial institutions often result in revenue-sharing agreements that benefit all parties. Platform can also monetize user data by providing business intelligence insights and targeted marketing services. In addition, the introduction of financial products such as loans, insurance, and investment options increases revenue and expands market reach.

CHAPTER 7

New Challenges in FinTech

Abstract This chapter examines the intersection of FinTech, AI, blockchain, and DeFi, exploring their implications, challenges, and regulatory considerations. It traces the evolution of AI, covering subsets such as ML and DL, as well as emerging technologies such as NLP and LLMs. The chapter highlights the transformative impact of AI on finance, including predictive analytics, algorithmic trading, credit scoring, fraud detection, and experimental applications of generative AI. DeFi challenges centralized financial systems by enabling decentralized payments, asset tokenization, and data verification. The chapter examines blockchain-driven innovations, including cryptocurrencies, stable coins, and smart contracts, and contrasts their decentralized potential with centralized exchanges and existing regulatory frameworks. It also looks at institutional resistance to DeFi and the regulatory hurdles that limit widespread adoption. Regulatory challenges remain a central theme, particularly the lack of global standards for AI and crypto assets. The chapter compares regulatory approaches in the EU, the US, and China, analyzing frameworks such as the EU AI Act and the Markets in Crypto Assets Regulation. It highlights the difficulties of regulating decentralized systems and the slow adaptation of financial authorities to emerging technologies. Finally, the chapter envisions a future in which FinTech innovations continue to disrupt traditional finance, depending on solving AI accountability issues, managing technological complexity,

T. Geçer and V. Akgiray, *The Financial Technology Revolution*,
https://doi.org/10.1007/978-3-031-92048-6_7

and overcoming institutional resistance to DeFi. It advocates for collaboration between legal and technological experts to fully realize FinTech's potential for societal benefit.

Keywords AI · ML · DL · Cryptocurrencies · Blockchain · Ethics · Regulations

7.1 A Brief Overview of Artificial Intelligence

AI has a long history, shaped by centuries of thought, research, and technological innovation. During the Middle Ages and Renaissance, pioneers such as Al-Khwarizmi, Al-Jazari, and Leonardo da Vinci developed mathematical models and mechanical devices that simulated human and animal actions. Al-Khwarizmi, known as the father of algebra, made fundamental contributions to mathematics; the term "algorithm" is derived from his name Al-Jazari, known as the "father of robotics," authored the book "The Book of Knowledge of Ingenious Mechanical Devices" (Kitab fi Ma'rifat al-Hiyal al-Handasiya), documenting original designs of hundreds of mechanical devices, largely imitating human anatomy. Leonardo da Vinci, a visionary in art, science, and engineering, designed machines inspired by human anatomy, many of which were ahead of their time. In the eighteenth and nineteenth centuries, mathematicians such as René Descartes and Gottfried Wilhelm Leibniz explored the integration of logic with numerical computation. Charles Babbage and Ada Lovelace envisioned a universal machine capable of computation and algorithmic operations, laying the foundation for modern computing.

The formal birth of AI began in the 1940s and 1950s with Claude Shannon's information theory and Alan Turing's Turing Test, which evaluated a machine's ability to exhibit intelligent behavior. The term "artificial intelligence" was officially introduced at the 1956 Dartmouth Conference in New Hampshire, marking the emergence of AI as a distinct field of study. Early AI systems such as Eliza, Mycin, and Shrdlu generated excitement by demonstrating basic reasoning and NLP capabilities in various domains. However, from the late 1960s to the early 1990s, a period known as the "AI winter," interest and funding for AI projects declined significantly. Despite this setback, researchers continued to solve complex problems, such as understanding the structure of the double helix, often relying on manual methods that later evolved into fundamental AI tools.

AI experienced a resurgence in the 1990s, driven by advances in computing technologies, digital communications, and the availability of data. This era marked the emergence of data science, a new discipline in computer science. Big data, which refers to massive data sets and the analysis of that data, enabled data scientists to collect, measure, analyze, and generate insights, pushing AI in new directions. AI systems, a subset of data science, use computer algorithms to mimic human intelligence by using big data to predict, automate, and optimize tasks. ML, a subset of AI, enables systems to learn from experience without explicit human intervention. In addition to processing new data, ML improves its capabilities by evaluating the results of previous algorithms and refining its performance over time. Historically, advances in ML have paralleled improvements in statistical methods, data science techniques, and computing power. The capabilities of ML were famously demonstrated by IBM's Deep Blue, which defeated chess champion Garry Kasparov in 1997, and DeepMind's AlphaGo, which triumphed over Lee Sedol in the complex game of Go in 2016.

Figure 7.1 shows the relationship between AI, ML, and DL in computer science and data science.

The increasing availability of large data sets and advances in computational algorithms-such as support vector machines and neural networks have driven the rise of DL, a subset of ML. DL uses multi-layered neural networks modeled after the human brain to process complex patterns and improve decision-making. The Turing Award, often referred to as the "Nobel Prize of Computing," is given annually by the Association for

Fig. 7.1 Intersection of AI, ML, and DL

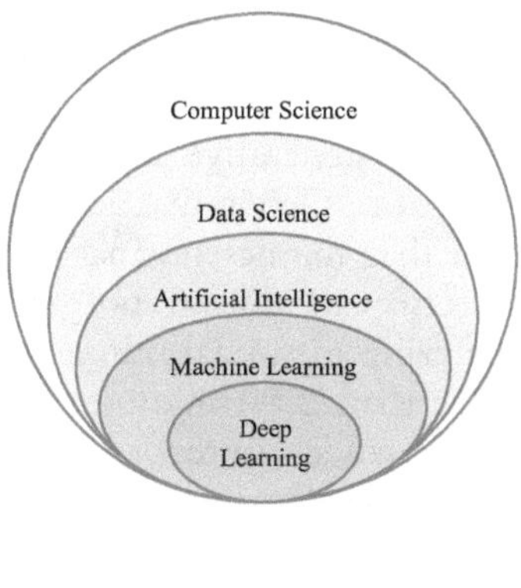

Computing Machinery to recognize groundbreaking contributions in the field of computing. Many winners have made significant advances in deep neural networks, solidifying DL as a cornerstone of modern AI.

DL, NLP, and LLM are transforming the way machines understand and generate human language. Technologies such as generative pre-trained transformers, bidirectional encoder representations of transformers, and virtual assistants such as Siri, Alexa, and Google Assistant exemplify the widespread adoption of these innovations. Researchers estimate that the progress of AI over the past two decades has been driven by exponential growth in computing power, which is increasing at a rate of about four times per year, and improvements in algorithmic efficiency, which are increasing at a rate of 2.5 times per year. As a result, the availability of adequate computing power has increased tenfold each year, underscoring the potential for AI to permeate all aspects of society. Recent focus of AI research is Artificial General Intelligence, an advanced form of AI capable of performing any intellectual task that a human can perform. Unlike narrow AI, which is designed for specific tasks, AGI aims to generalize problem-solving abilities without the need for task-specific training.

7.2 Artificial Intelligence in Finance

Despite technological advances, AI lacks a universally accepted definition for policymaking and regulation. From an ethical and societal perspective, it is important to distinguish between predictive and generative AI, as they serve different functions—particularly in the financial sector. Predictive AI uses statistical techniques to analyze large data sets, identifying historical patterns to predict future market parameters. Because it relies solely on historical data, most financial AI applications fall into this category. In contrast, generative AI uses data training techniques to create synthetic data, including text, images, and media. Although still experimental in finance, generative adversarial networks have shown promise in fraud detection. Generative adversarial networks generate synthetic transaction data that mimics normal user behavior. Deviations from these synthetic patterns can indicate potential fraud, while predictive AI detects fraud by analyzing historical transaction patterns. The financial industry generates more than 2.5 trillion gigabytes of big data every day, including market data, transaction records, corporate disclosures, and social media insights. Given the demand for efficiency, integrity, and accessibility, finance is a prime sector for AI-driven innovation. However, the adoption of AI in finance has been slow, with most applications still in development. Two key factors are holding back the adoption of AI in finance.

- Lack of Global AI Regulations: Currently, there is no universal framework for AI, and many countries need to develop their own national AI policies. The lack of standardized regulations creates uncertainty and slows the integration of AI into financial markets.
- Strict Financial Regulations: The financial industry enforces strict requirements to ensure market integrity, consumer protection, financial stability, risk management, privacy, and system governance. These regulatory obligations often conflict with the rapid evolution of AI, particularly generative AI models, which necessitate adaptive oversight frameworks.

This regulatory friction has led to the "explainability problem," where AI algorithms are often too complex for humans to fully interpret. In response, explainable artificial intelligence aims to improve the transparency and interpretability of AI, although it is still a work in progress. Despite these challenges, the adoption of AI in finance is expected to accelerate as regulatory clarity improves. Similar to other digital financial technologies, AI is likely to follow a similar trajectory in product development and industry integration. This chapter explores key AI applications in finance, recognizing that the future of AI-powered FinTech may look very different from its current state as the technology evolves, and regulations adapt.

Trading and Asset Management

As computing power has increased, trading models and algorithms have become more sophisticated and data-driven. In the early 2000s, high-frequency trading algorithms emerged that were capable of executing large trade orders in milliseconds (10^{-3} seconds) or nanoseconds (10^{-9} seconds). These algorithms exploit temporary market inefficiencies and small price discrepancies to generate profits. In recent years, AI-driven trading models have evolved to integrate market data and social media analytics, significantly improving their predictive capabilities. Today, algorithmic trading accounts for approximately 80% of total trading volume on U.S. exchanges. On smaller exchanges, such as Borsa Istanbul, it is around 30% and growing.

Algorithmic trading systems offers several key advantages:

- Speed and Efficiency: They process both structured and unstructured data in fractions of a second, enabling faster transactions.
- Improved Risk and Liquidity Management: AI optimizes market exposure and increases liquidity.
- Large Order Execution: These systems increase the efficiency of order flow and transaction management.

However, there are inherent risks, including:

- Herding Behavior: AI-driven trading can lead to one-sided markets characterized by excessive momentum.
- Illiquidity Under Stress: Flash crashes can occur during periods of market stress due to rapid order execution failures.
- Increased Market Volatility: AI can amplify price fluctuations by reacting quickly to market events.
- Risks of Market Manipulation: Machine-to-machine interactions can enable spoofing and collusion.

AI-based models can identify trading signals and uncover complex relationships in large data sets, providing numerous competitive advantages:

- Streamlined Operations: AI improves algorithmic trading and optimizes the routing of small orders.
- Advanced Risk Management: AI enhances pattern recognition, stress testing, market sentiment analysis, and continuous portfolio optimization.
- Personalized Client Strategies: AI enables preference-based investment strategies based on individual preferences and offers chatbot-based advisory services.

AI development is costly due to the high computing power and large data requirements it requires, which tends to favor larger financial institutions. This can lead to:

- Market Concentration: Smaller firms may find it difficult to compete, leading to a reduction in market diversity.
- Strategy Convergence: Widespread adoption of similar AI models on comparable data sets can stifle innovation.
- The Explainability Problem: 'Black box' AI algorithms are difficult to explain to clients and regulators.

AI models in algorithmic trading and asset management primarily fall under the category of predictive AI. High-frequency trading has gained significant market share and is widely used by both institutional and retail traders. However, the adoption of AI in asset management remains uneven. Active asset managers are increasingly integrating AI into their investment strategies for risk analysis, portfolio optimization, and automated decision-making. In contrast, passive managers, who follow market trends without frequent rebalancing, generally avoid AI tools. Despite the potential of generative AI, passive management continues to resist AI adoption. Over the past decade, the ratio of passive to active portfolios has increased from less than 50% to more than 120%. Yet the asset management industry has yet to fully embrace AI, indicating a continued reliance on traditional investment strategies. Hedge funds, which frequently adjust their investment strategies, have benefited significantly from AI. AI-driven hedge funds have consistently outperformed traditional hedge funds because AI is more efficient than human traders at identifying short-term risks and opportunities.

Risk Management and Compliance

AI-based credit scoring assesses creditworthiness by analyzing large amounts of structured and unstructured data, including social media behavior, past payment history, and transactional information. Unlike traditional credit scoring, which relies on a limited set of financial and demographic data, AI-based models offer greater accuracy, flexibility, and comprehensiveness.

- Increased Financial Inclusion: AI expands access to credit for underserved populations, including small businesses and individuals with limited or no credit history.

- Fraud Detection and Risk Assessment: ML-powered real-time analytics quickly identify high-risk borrowers by detecting suspicious activity and fraud patterns.
- Faster Credit Decisions: AI improves operational efficiency and user satisfaction by providing instant or near-instant approvals.

FinTech companies and BigTech platforms, such as Amazon and Alibaba, are offering AI-based credit scoring services. At the same time, traditional financial institutions are either engaging directly or partnering with FinTechs. Major concern with AI-based credit scoring is the potential to amplify biases and produce discriminatory outcomes if models are not carefully designed. Explanatory artificial intelligence can help mitigate this issue by increasing transparency and fairness in the decision-making process. Given the highly regulated nature of the financial industry, ensuring regulatory compliance is both complex and costly. The challenge lies in navigating an evolving landscape of detailed financial regulations. In the field of RegTech, AI tools are particularly well-suited to address this regulatory complexity by automating compliance and risk assessment.

- Automated Compliance Analysis: ML and NLP algorithms quickly interpret laws and regulations and generate customized reports and recommendations for compliance teams.
- Regulatory Tracking: NLP tools identify new regulations and changes, triggering updates to internal risk management policies.
- KYC Compliance: AI streamlines KYC processes by analyzing multiple sources of user data to ensure thorough verification.
- AML and Anti-Terrorist Financing: AI monitors financial transactions in real-time, detecting anomalies, and suspicious behavior to improve regulatory compliance.
- Automated Auditing: AI simplifies the audit process by generating compliance reports and comparing them to historical data to identify discrepancies in real-time.

Beyond financial institutions, regulators and supervisors are also using AI for enforcement and surveillance, a practice known as supervisory technology. ML and NLP help detect and prevent money laundering, illicit financing, and market abuse in near real-time. Securities regulators in several countries have implemented AI-based surveillance systems to detect market manipulation and insider trading. By analyzing real-time transaction data and social media activity, these systems can detect organized network behavior, representing an emerging application of AI in financial supervision.

Credit Intermediation

AI-driven credit scoring has extended credit underwriting to SMEs, micro-SMEs, and individuals with limited credit histories. FinTech companies such as Rocket Mortgage, LendingClub, and Revolut now serve millions of borrowers and have established themselves as leaders in specific market segments. In 2022, LendingClub reported 3 million users with an average loan size of $16,000-an amount often overlooked by traditional lenders. Rocket Mortgage, originally founded in the 1980s as a technology provider to banks, transformed after the 2008 financial crisis into a retail mortgage lender targeting first-time homebuyers and those with lower credit scores. Today, it is the largest retail mortgage lender in the U.S. Similar trend is emerging in BigTech lending. Amazon Lending is expanding into small business financing, serving both marketplace sellers and outside small businesses. Apple has entered lending space with the Apple Card and BNPL services, while Alibaba offers loans through its Huabei and Jiebei platforms, and other BigTech companies operate similar lending services. Given the current regulatory landscape, FinTech and BigTech lenders need to partner with banks to ensure compliance and leverage banking infrastructure. However, as these companies obtain independent banking licenses, they could disrupt traditional banking models and accelerate the shift toward "banking without banks."

With the exception of certain internal generative AI projects, the use of AI in credit intermediation relies primarily on predictive models. However, challenges related to tractability and regulatory complexity make it difficult to develop fully automated credit models without human oversight. This is particularly true in straightforward cases where transparency is essential for regulatory compliance. Consequently, despite AI's ability to process large amounts of data and generate lending recommendations, human intervention remains critical for final lending decisions. As a result, AI-based lending still represents a small share of overall lending market. Beyond lending, AI is revolutionizing personalized financial planning through robo-advisory services. Following developments in portfolio management and trading, AI is now being used to customize investment strategies for individual investors. Robo-advisor is an algorithm-driven financial planner that evaluates an investor's financial profile, including income, assets, risk tolerance, goals, and behavioral characteristics. Based on this information, it constructs and monitors investment portfolios and dynamically adjusts allocations as needed.

AI-powered robo-advisors offer several key benefits, including faster decision-making, lower costs, and greater accessibility for retail investors. AI is expected to revolutionize robo-advisory services by increasing personalization, identifying behavioral patterns, and improving efficiency. While AI has automated and streamlined financial planning, its full potential continues to evolve as it is further integrated into financial ecosystem. Despite initial enthusiasm, the momentum for AI-driven financial advice has slowed in recent years due to several factors. AI is already embedded in portfolio design, with mutual funds tailored to different investor profiles and risk-return preferences. Wealthy individuals seeking customized portfolios and professional oversight often rely on wealth managers and family offices, where human interaction remains essential. In contrast, retail investors are often considered too small to warrant extensive personalization, while wealthy clients can afford traditional human advisory services. Recent OECD study (2024) highlights the growing role of AI in financial services across firms, product categories, and use cases.

- By company, banks (49%) lead in AI use, followed by insurance companies (42%), asset managers (39%), securities firms (34%), non-bank financial institutions (28%), regulators (29%), and other financial firms (20%).
- By product category, AI is primarily used in banking and payments (35%), credit intermediation (33%), financial advice (27%), insurance underwriting (24%), and trading (18%).
- Common AI Applications: The most common AI use cases include customer relationship management (50%), process automation (47%), fraud detection (39%), data analytics (29%), risk management and compliance (28%), portfolio management (23%), cybersecurity (15%), and supervisory technology (SupTech) (9%).

As generative AI technology advances and governance frameworks evolve to address accountability concerns, the role of AI in finance is expected to expand significantly. Similar growth is expected in industries beyond finance.

7.3 Decentralized Finance and Blockchain

The traditional financial system operates as a centralized network, commonly referred to as CeFi. In this model, all monetary transactions and capital flows between individuals and companies are facilitated by intermediaries regulated by central authorities. The primary function of the financial system is to facilitate intermediation between capital providers (savers and investors) and capital seekers (borrowers, companies, and governments). Major financial intermediaries include commercial banks, investment banks, securities firms, mutual funds, asset managers, and insurance companies. Intermediate action occurs through direct placements or in money and capital markets, with banking and securities regulators establishing and enforcing regulatory frameworks under government authority. Central banks influence the money supply, often indirectly through the banking system, while fiscal authorities oversee government budgets, taxation, and public finances. The global financial system faces several key challenges that have intensified criticism of the CeFi model.

Since the 1980s, the world has experienced a rise in both the frequency and severity of financial crises. This trend has prompted significant criticism of the financial system. Several issues have been identified in the financial sector.

- Concentrated control and ownership by a limited number of financial institutions is evident; for example, in the United Kingdom, over 50% of deposits are held by the four largest banks.
- Low efficiency and high cost of intermediation, as evidenced by the fact that banks' total payments revenue exceeds $2.2 trillion per year (McKinsey, 2023).
- Complex products, opaque governance, and interoperability barriers.
- More than 1.5 billion people lack access to financial services.

High costs and barriers to entry in traditional finance have slowed economic growth and exacerbated inequality. DeFi emerged as a potential solution, inspired by Satoshi Nakamoto's 2008 white paper. In that paper, Nakamoto proposed "a new electronic money system that is completely peer-to-peer, with no trusted third-party, using Bitcoin as its currency. Although Bitcoin was originally designed as a peer-to-peer payment system without intermediaries, its underlying blockchain technology has become a foundation for DeFi. Some political economists view the creation of Bitcoin as an act of defiance against the socially unethical roots of the 2008 financial crisis. Blockchain is a decentralized, peer-to-peer network that confirms transactions and transfers ownership without intermediaries or a central authority. It is based on distributed ledger technology, cryptography, and smart contracts. Unlike traditional bank ledgers, which rely on centralized record-keeping, a DLT-based system distributes records across multiple nodes, increasing security, transparency, and efficiency.

Figure 7.2 compares the structures and interactions of centralized and decentralized ledgers and illustrates how data is managed in each system.

In a centralized ledger system, each customer maintains an individual ledger, while the bank maintains the general ledger, known as the "golden ledger." All transactions, including user payments, are processed through the bank as an intermediary, requiring reconciliation between users and the bank. As a regulated entity, the bank is responsible for securing, verifying, and establishing trust in financial transactions. In contrast, a blockchain operates as a decentralized system, eliminating the need for a central authority. Transactions are verified across a distributed network

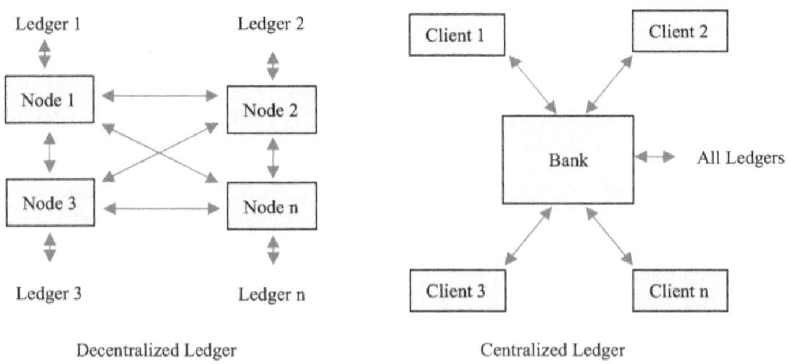

Fig. 7.2 Decentralized vs. centralized ledgers

using cryptographic validation, rather than relying on a single intermediary. Standard blockchain follows a structured, sequential process to ensure security, transparency, and decentralization.

1. Transaction Initiation: Node initiates a transaction (e.g., sending money) and broadcasts it to the network. The transaction is secured using asymmetric cryptography.
    - A public key encrypts the data and makes it accessible to the network.
    - A private key, known only to the initiator of the transaction, is used to decrypt the data.
2. Transaction Validation: The network verifies the validity of a transaction by ensuring that sufficient funds are available, and that the transaction adheres to a consensus algorithm, such as Proof of Work or Proof of Stake. This process establishes trust and helps prevent fraud.
3. Block Creation and Security: Validated transactions are recorded in a new block that is cryptographically linked to the previous block. Hash function converts the transaction data into a fixed-size hexadecimal string, ensuring data integrity. Once a block is added:
    - Tampering becomes computationally impossible because changing a block requires decrypting its hash and recalculating all subsequent hashes.
    - The blockchain remains immutable, ensuring that a single, verifiable version cannot be altered.

Satoshi Nakamoto's Bitcoin system is widely regarded as the first actual blockchain, fully embodying the principles of decentralization, cryptographic security, and peer-to-peer transactions. In Satoshi's words, Bitcoin is a "new open-source P2P e-cash system" that eliminates the need for central servers or trusted third-parties, relying instead on cryptographic proof. What Bitcoin calls "e-cash" or "Bitcoin" is classified as "money" or "currency" in traditional finance. Because Bitcoin operates without a central bank, new coins-called "cryptocurrency" are created as monetary rewards for miners, who validate transactions through a process known as mining.

Initially, the Bitcoin blockchain served primarily as a decentralized payment system. However, the introduction of smart contracts on the Ethereum blockchain marked a significant advancement. Smart contract is a self-executing agreement between parties that does not require an intermediary, such as a lawyer, to enforce its terms. These contracts are encoded as immutable computer programs and operate autonomously on a blockchain network. In finance, most assets, such as stocks and bonds, exist as legal contracts, while trading relies on agreements between buyers and sellers. This innovative contract technology enables both financial and non-financial assets to be created and exchanged directly on the blockchain. These assets, known as "tokenized assets" or simply "tokens," are the foundation of DeFi and blockchain-based trading. Two key observations highlight the connection between blockchain technology and real-world economics.

- Technologies such as TCP/IP, HTML, and HTTP enabled the creation of internet and facilitated the transfer of asset-based information. This evolution has led to the emergence of centralized, platform-based business models, such as Amazon, which have transformed commerce. This era is commonly referred to as Web 2.0.

4. Technologies such as cryptography, smart contracts, and distributed ledgers enable blockchain to facilitate the transfer of value (or ownership) of assets. This advancement is expected to lead to decentralized, open business models that are both disruptive and foundational. The term of web 3.0 is used here to indicate a new direction for FinTech development.

Blockchain technologies can be classified into different types based on their access and permission structures (Akgiray, 2019). These classifications, ranked in order of decreasing similarity to Satoshi Nakamoto's original design, are as follows.

1. Open Blockchains

    - Public Permissionless: Anyone can read, write, and perform transactions. Examples include Bitcoin and Ethereum.

- Public Permissioned: Anyone can read, but only authorized nodes can write and execute transactions. Example: a public supply chain ledger.

2. Closed Blockchains

- Consortium: Only authorized nodes can read, write, and commit transactions. For example, a shared ledger maintained by multiple banks.
- Private Permissioned: Only authorized nodes can read, and only the network operator can write and commit transactions. For example, a bank ledger shared between a parent company and its subsidiary.

Often integrated with smart contracts, blockchain technology has been widely adopted across various industries. Most implementations operate as public permissioned blockchains or consortium networks. The following is a summary of key applications:

Supply Chain and Logistics: Improves traceability, prevents fraud and counterfeiting, and reduces processing time.
Healthcare: Secures patient data, ensures transparency in clinical trial results, and manages the pharmaceutical supply chain.
Public Services: Facilitate real estate transactions, digital identity verification, voting systems, credential verification (e.g., school transcripts), notary services, and aid distribution.
Internet of Things: Supports device authentication, data sharing, and real-time automation in smart homes and autonomous vehicles.
Media and Gaming: Protects digital rights, facilitates tokenized in-game assets, and enables the trading of digital art through NFTs.
Energy and Carbon Markets: Certification of renewable energy and tokenization of energy-related digital assets.

Given the origins of the concept, finance has proven to be the most fertile ground for blockchain adoption.

Cross-Border Payments: The financial industry represents a prime opportunity for blockchain adoption, particularly in cross-border payments. This market is immense, with total transaction flows exceeding $150 trillion and net revenues exceeding $250 billion by 2022 (McKinsey, 2023). Despite some technological advances, the legacy global payments system remains inefficient, burdened by high costs, slow processing times, and monopolistic structures. These inefficiencies stem from multiple layers of banking intermediation and reliance on SWIFT, the dominant centralized messaging infrastructure for international transactions.

Several companies are exploring blockchain-based solutions to streamline cross-border payments and eliminate intermediary friction. Ripple is a blockchain-based, peer-to-peer payment system that facilitates international transactions without intermediaries. It is an on-demand liquidity technology that uses the Ripple token as a bridge currency for real-time settlements. Ripple's key benefits include (a) transaction speed: settlements are completed in 3–5 seconds, compared to hours or even days with SWIFT; (b) lower cost: Transaction fees are measured in cents, significantly cheaper than legacy systems that charge approximately 2% per transaction; and (c) enhanced security: End-to-end encryption ensures secure transactions and reduces the risk of fraud. Despite regulatory uncertainty, more than 300 financial institutions in 22 countries have adopted Ripple's blockchain technology. However, it remains a small player with a transaction volume of less than 1% of the global market, compared to SWIFT's network of approximately 11,000 institutions in over 200 countries. Nevertheless, Ripple poses a potentially disruptive threat to traditional financial networks, especially if regulatory challenges are resolved. Beyond Ripple, other FinTech companies such as Wise are expanding into blockchain-based cross-border payments, signaling a broader industry shift toward decentralized, real-time payment solutions.

Crypto Activity: Crypto assets are digital or virtual assets issued and traded on blockchains or distributed networks. Unlike traditional finance, which relies on regulated intermediaries to establish trust, cryptosystems use cryptographic methods to ensure security, transparency, and integrity. The term covers all platforms, exchanges, and decentralized applications where crypto assets are traded, exchanged, or used. While there is no universally accepted classification for crypto assets, a rapidly expanding financial ecosystem—including FinTechs, DeFi protocols, and traditional financial institutions—is actively developing around them.

- Tokens: Tokens serve several functions in blockchain ecosystems: (1) Utility and Governance Tokens: Provide access to blockchain services and voting rights for system upgrades. Examples: Chainlink, which connects smart contracts to real-world data, and Uniswap, which allows users to participate in governance decisions. (2) Security Tokens: Represent fractional ownership of financial or physical assets, such as real estate, company shares, or debt instruments. (3) Non-Fungible Tokens: Represent unique digital assets, including art, collectibles, in-game items, and intellectual property rights. Tokenization is also expanding into waste management and carbon credit markets, creating new economic opportunities.

- Stablecoins: Stablecoins are crypto assets that are pegged to external values, such as fiat currencies, commodities, or other cryptocurrencies, thus providing price stability compared to volatile cryptocurrencies. There are three main types of stablecoins: (1) Fiat-pegged stablecoins: These are backed 1:1 by fiat currency reserves and can be redeemed at face value at any time. Examples include Tether and USD Coin, which are fully backed by cash reserves and short-term U.S. Treasury bills. (2) Commodity-linked stablecoins: Their value fluctuates based on the price of an underlying asset, typically a precious metal or other tangible commodity. An example is Pax Gold, which is tied to the price of gold and allows investors to hold tokenized digital gold. (3) Crypto-backed stable coins: These are backed by other cryptocurrencies, often over-collate to mitigate market volatility. An example is DAI, issued by MakerDAO, which is backed by Ethereum and other digital assets through collateralized debt obligations. As of December 2024, the total market value of stablecoins was approximately $208 billion, reflecting continued growth and increased adoption in DeFi and cross-border payments.
- Cryptocurrencies: Cryptocurrencies are unbacked digital assets designed to function as decentralized money, issued peer-to-peer without a central authority. Unlike fiat currencies, which are the foundation of CeFi and are regulated by central banks, cryptocurrencies operate independently in blockchain networks. Bitcoin, the most prominent cryptocurrency, performs the three essential functions of money: (1) medium of exchange, (2) store of value, and (3) unit of account. However, unlike fiat currencies, Bitcoin is not issued by a central bank or legally authorized entity. Instead, it is generated through mining, which relies on proof-of-work consensus mechanisms to validate transactions and secure the network.

As of December 2024, the total cryptocurrency market capitalization is $3.85 trillion, with over 16,000 digital assets traded on 1,190 exchanges.

Cryptocurrencies dominate this market, accounting for $3.6 trillion of the total. Bitcoin, valued at $2.1 trillion, and Ethereum, valued at $470 billion, are the two largest cryptocurrencies, together accounting for 72% of the market share. Bitcoin, which began trading in 2009, reached a market cap of $500 billion in 2021 and has experienced significant growth since then. Cryptocurrency prices are highly correlated and volatile and are primarily traded on global digital exchanges that operate around the clock. Both specialized crypto brokers and traditional brokerage platforms now provide access to these markets. There are two main types of cryptocurrency exchanges.

- DEXs facilitate peer-to-peer cryptocurrency and trading on blockchain platforms like Ethereum, using smart contracts to eliminate intermediaries. Popular DEXs include Radium, Uniswap, Sushiswap, and PancakeSwap. However, trading volumes on DEXs remain lower than on centralized exchanges.
- CEXs function similarly to traditional financial exchanges, with centralized management and intermediary brokers overseeing transactions. Unlike DEXs, CEXs operate trading platforms directly, rather than using the blockchain itself. As of 2024, the largest CEXs by trading volume include:
  - Binance: Based in the Cayman Islands, Binance is the largest crypto exchange in the world, with a daily spot trading volume of approximately $15 billion.
  - Bybit: Headquartered in Dubai, Bybit offers spot and derivatives trading with a daily volume of approximately $4.5 billion.
  - Coinbase: Headquartered in San Francisco, regulated public company in the USA with a daily trade volume of about $3 billion.

In addition to the 400 million individuals who own or trade cryptocurrencies, key market participants include FinTech companies, crypto asset developers, and traditional financial institutions. Goldman Sachs has launched several exchange-traded funds and cryptocurrency derivatives. The Chicago Mercantile Exchange offers a wide range of crypto derivatives, while Lloyd's is integrating crypto derivatives into its insurance products. Payment providers such as PayPal and Visa have integrated tokens and stable coins into their payment infrastructures. Despite a projected market capitalization of $4 trillion by 2024, crypto assets still account for less than 1% of the $500 trillion global financial market. This disparity is due to a lack of smooth integration with traditional finance, and the underlying technology remains complex for most users. However, the accelerating adoption of cryptocurrencies signals a potential shift in the financial landscape.

7.4 Regulation of FinTech

Financial regulation refers to the legal framework established by governments and independent authorities to ensure the stability and integrity of financial institutions and markets. Its main objectives include.

- Consumer Protection: Protecting consumers from fraud and operational risks.
- Market Efficiency: Ensuring that financial markets are fair, competitive, and transparent.
- Financial Crime Prevention: Detecting and combating money laundering, illegal activities, and terrorist financing.
- Trust and Confidence: Strengthening public trust and confidence in financial markets promotes economic growth.
- Financial Stability: Monitoring and mitigating systemic risks to prevent financial crises.

Financial regulation is enforced by national and international regulatory bodies that oversee banking, securities, and insurance. These international institutions set global financial standards to ensure stability and compliance. Major international financial standards include:

- The Basel Committee on Banking Supervision sets global banking standards.
- The International Organization of Securities Commissions regulates securities markets.
- International Association of Insurance Supervisors sets insurance industry standards.
- The Financial Action Task Force develops standards for AML and CTF.

- International Financial Reporting Standards Board sets financial reporting standards.

In addition, organizations such as the World Bank and the OECD provide guidance and policy recommendations on financial regulation and economic policy. The following section summarizes the national regulators and supervisors in major economies.

EU: Financial regulation and supervision in the EU primarily occur at the Union level, covering all 28 Member States. However, national authorities are responsible for supervising local and smaller financial institutions to ensure compliance with EU rules. While supervisory framework is decentralized, it remains highly harmonized.

- Banking Regulation: The European Banking Authority sets regulatory standards, while the European Central Bank supervises systemically important banks under the Single Supervisory Mechanism.
- Securities Regulation: The European Securities and Markets Authority oversees all securities markets in the EU, while national authorities are responsible for ensuring compliance with regulations.
- Insurance Regulation: The European Insurance and Occupational Pensions Authority is the primary regulator of the insurance sector in the EU.

United States: The U.S. regulatory framework is fragmented across federal and state agencies, often resulting in jurisdictional disputes. Despite this complexity, federal banking and securities regulators play a critical role in shaping the global influence of the U.S. financial industry and maintaining the dominance of the U.S. dollar in international finance.

- Banking Regulation: Fed supervises bank and thrift holding companies, Fed member banks, and foreign banks operating in the U.S. The Office of the Comptroller of the Currency regulates national banks and thrifts, while state banking agencies supervise state-chartered banks.
- Securities Regulation: The Securities and Exchange Commission regulates all securities markets, with the exception of derivatives markets, which are overseen by the Commodity Futures Trading Commission.

- Insurance Regulation: Each state regulates insurance independently, with voluntary coordination facilitated by the National Association of Insurance Commissioners.

China: China's financial regulation operates in a centrally controlled framework designed to achieve national economic objectives. Laws and regulations are enacted at the national level, with banking and securities authorities responsible for supervision and enforcement, coordinated by central commissions.

- Banking Regulation: The PBOC is China's central bank and supervises the financial system. The China Banking and Insurance Regulatory Commission is responsible for supervising banks, regional financial institutions, and insurance companies.
- Securities Regulation: The China Securities Regulatory Commission is responsible for overseeing and regulating securities markets and institutions.
- Insurance Regulation: China Banking and Insurance Regulatory Commission is the primary regulator of China's insurance sector.

Because FinTech products and services operate in the financial sector, their regulation falls under general financial laws rather than a separate framework. New payment systems and digital banking models that use fiat currencies remain integrated into the existing economic and monetary system. While these innovations increase efficiency and accessibility, their basic structure is similar to traditional finance, making regulation relatively straightforward. PSD2 is a comprehensive EU regulation for payment systems and service providers. It mandates the use of open banking APIs that allow banks and PSPs to access users' payment accounts. Regulatory oversight is provided by the European Central Bank and the European Banking Authority, in coordination with national regulators. Access methods must comply with GDPR to ensure data privacy and security. An updated version, known as PSD3, is under development.

Fed, the Office of the Comptroller of the Currency and state regulators regulate payment services in the US. Unlike the EU, Open Banking is not mandatory, and the provision of APIs is driven by market forces. The Electronic Fund Transfer Act and the Gramm-Leach-Bliley Act provide for consumer protection, privacy, and security. Major private PSPs include Visa, Mastercard, and emerging FinTech companies.

China's payment infrastructure is highly advanced but remains tightly controlled by the PBOC. While open banking is allowed, all transaction data must be stored in PBOC systems, prioritizing data centralization over privacy. Leading private PSPs include Alipay and WeChat Pay. Payment regulations in Japan and Singapore are similar to those in the EU, but allow for more market-driven innovation, including blockchain-based payment models. These countries have adapted to technological advances faster than most. In addition, both countries prioritize cross-border regulatory harmonization, fostering a more integrated global payments landscape. The regulation of crypto assets, decentralized systems, and AI-driven finance has been slow and complex due to incompatibilities with traditional financial regulatory frameworks. Existing financial regulation is based on three core pillars, and the absence of any one of them challenges the traditional regulatory model.

1. Dependence on Intermediaries: Financial regulation relies on intermediations that serve as central points for supervision and enforcement. However, existing regulatory frameworks are not designed to regulate decentralized systems that operate without intermediaries.
2. Jurisdictional Challenges: Traditional financial regulations apply in specific national or regional boundaries. In contrast, decentralized financial systems and crypto assets operate across global networks, creating enforcement and compliance challenges for regulators.
3. Evolving Regulatory Jurisdiction: As technology replaces human decision-making, regulatory frameworks must adapt to establish clear accountability, oversight, and enforcement mechanisms in an increasingly automated financial system.

Artificial Intelligence

International and national authorities have published cross-sectoral policy reports on AI regulation, with most adopting the OECD's definition of AI: "An AI system is a machine-based system that, for explicit or implicit purposes, infers from the input it receives how to produce outputs such as predictions, content, recommendations, or decisions that can affect physical or virtual environments. AI systems vary in their autonomy and adaptability once deployed" (OECD, 2024). Policy recommendations typically emphasize privacy and data protection, security and reliability, accountability, transparency, fairness, and ethics. The EU AI Act (2024) introduces a risk-based regulatory framework that classifies AI systems according to their perceived risks.

- Unacceptable Risk: AI systems that are deemed harmful or that violate basic human rights will be prohibited. Examples include government social scoring and manipulative AI.
- High Risk: The use of AI in sensitive sectors such as healthcare, finance, employment, and law enforcement will be subject to strict regulations. These requirements include comprehensive risk management, bias prevention using high-quality data, traceability for compliance purposes, and human oversight where necessary. Most obligations apply to developers, with fewer requirements for deployers.
- Limited Risk: AI applications, such as chatbots, must comply with transparency regulations and inform users that they are interacting with AI.
- Minimal Risk: The use of AI in non-sensitive contexts, such as video games, remains unregulated.

AI regulation in the US remains underdeveloped compared to the EU AI Act. While some sector-specific guidelines exist, they are largely market-driven and voluntary and focus primarily on data privacy. In contrast, China has adopted a centralized regulatory approach, emphasizing government oversight as part of its ambition to become a global leader in AI. Currently, there is no international consensus on AI regulation, and most existing laws focus on predictive AI models. However, generative AI introduces new complexities that future regulations will need to address, a challenging task given the rapid evolution of AI technology. Common AI policy issues, such as governance, risk management, and investor protection, are consistent with existing financial regulations. As a result, most governments have not implemented AI-specific regulations for the financial sector, opting instead to adapt general AI frameworks for financial applications. Only a few jurisdictions, including

Qatar and certain U.S. states, have enacted AI-specific financial regulations (Crisanto et al., 2024). Given the rapid advancement of AI and its increasing adoption in financial services, monetary authorities may soon need to revise existing regulations.

Regulation of Crypto Activities

Regulating crypto activity remains challenging due to the lack of a universal taxonomy and the diverse nature of crypto assets. While some advanced economies are moving quickly to implement regulations, others are lagging behind. Meanwhile, some emerging markets are attempting to stifle crypto activity through outright bans, citing concerns about currency substitution and capital outflows. Even among progressive jurisdictions, regulatory approaches vary, complicating the management of cross-border crypto transactions—a core feature of digital assets. The EU, Japan and Singapore have enacted some of the most comprehensive crypto regulations. Japan amended its Payment Services Act (originally enacted in 2009) in 2016 and 2020 to regulate crypto assets, placing them under the jurisdiction of Financial Services Agency. Singapore regulates crypto markets under the Payment Services Act (2019), which is overseen by the Monetary Authority of Singapore. The EU adopted the Markets in Crypto Assets Regulation (2023), which came into force in 2024, establishing a single framework for supervision of crypto assets. The following section outlines common asset classifications and regulatory standards across jurisdictions.

- Covered Assets: Stablecoins backed by fiat currencies or other assets, as well as utility and governance tokens, are subject to regulation. Security tokens are excluded from this classification as they are considered traditional financial securities.
- Regulatory Requirements: Strict standards for licensing, custody, redemption reserves, audits, and risk management must be followed.
- AML and KYC Compliance: Mandatory AML, CTF, and KYC protocols are enforced.
- Exchange Restrictions: Trading platforms are prohibited from trading on their own behalf or listing tokens that they have issued.
- Unbacked Cryptocurrencies: Bitcoin, Ethereum, and other unbacked cryptocurrencies are not directly regulated. However,

cryptocurrency exchanges must comply with strict licensing requirements.
- Legal Status of Cryptocurrencies: While cryptocurrencies are not recognized as legal tender, commercial transactions involving them are permitted if both parties agree.

Crypto regulation in the U.S. is fragmented and primarily enforcement-driven, lacking a comprehensive federal framework. The Securities and Exchange Commission and the Commodity Futures Trading Commission disagree on whether crypto assets should be classified as securities or commodities. Meanwhile, the Internal Revenue Service classifies them as property for tax purposes. Some states, including New York and California, are enforcing their own regulations. Cryptocurrencies can be traded freely, and crypto exchanges, such as Coinbase, operate under SEC licensing requirements similar to those for traditional exchanges. The Financial Crimes Enforcement Network enforces AML and CTF regulations.

China enforces strict regulations on crypto assets, prohibiting most related activities. In 2021, the PBOC imposed a comprehensive ban on cryptocurrency trading, exchange services, and foreign platforms targeting Chinese users. As a result, major exchanges such as Binance and Bybit moved their operations overseas. Prior to the ban, China accounted for over 70% of global cryptocurrency mining, but by late 2021, the majority of these operations had moved to the U.S., Kazakhstan, and Russia. The ban on private cryptocurrencies is in line with China's initiative to promote the digital yuan, a CBDC issued by the PBOC.

7.5 Future of FinTech

Recent regulatory developments are summarized across countries in the CCAF (2024) and BIS reports (Crisanto et al., 2024). Two major trends have emerged.

- Regulations are primarily focused on specific tokens and stable coins, while tokenized financial assets and tokenization process receive little attention. The term "cryptocurrency" is increasingly rare in regulatory texts.

- While centralized cryptocurrency exchanges are increasingly regulated, blockchain technology and DeFi continue to operate in a largely unregulated environment. The conceptual framework for regulating DeFi is still in its early stages of development.

The traditional financial system is resistant to disruption due to the structural integration of banking, money, and payments. Approximately 90% of the global money supply is generated through deposits and loans. Banks serve as the backbone of both domestic and cross-border payments, reinforcing their institutional power while increasing systemic fragility. As a result, financial regulation primarily emphasizes sustainability measures, including capital requirements, deposit insurance, and lender-of-last-resort facilities. James Tobin (1985) highlighted the inherent tension between economic power and fragility and suggested that separating banking functions from money creation and payments could reduce systemic risks. However, resistance to such structural changes remains strong. Notable example is the stablecoin Libra, later rebranded as Diem, which was introduced by Facebook in 2019. Designed to operate on a public, permissioned blockchain, it was backed by fiat currency and managed by a consortium of major financial institutions, including Visa, Mastercard, and PayPal. With Meta's billions of users, Diem was positioned as the first large-scale private digital currency.

By 2021, regulatory pushback led to the cancelation of the project. Governments and central banks raised concerns about financial stability, money laundering, data privacy, and threats to sovereign currencies. Fundamentally, Libra challenged the traditional banking model by attempting to separate payments from conventional banking-a move perceived as a direct threat to central bank control over monetary policy. Although Libra ultimately failed, it sparked a global conversation about the future of money and accelerated the development of CBDCs. CBDC is a digital version of a country's currency, issued and regulated by its central bank. Various CBDC models have been proposed, ranging from token-based systems that provide complete anonymity (similar to cash), to account-based systems that provide no anonymity, to hybrid models that provide partial anonymity. According to the Atlantic Council's CBDC Tracker, of 134 central banks, 44 are running pilot programs, 20 are developing models, and 39 are conducting research. Three countries-Nigeria, the Bahamas, and Jamaica-have already established CBDCs, while others remain inactive.

Most central banks prefer a wholesale, account-based CBDC model in which banks and financial institutions act as intermediaries, managing accounts and clearing and settling transactions. The central bank's reserve accounting remains unchanged. Since 95% of the world's money supply is already digital, this model closely resembles the existing financial system, making it more of a marketing initiative than a true innovation. Rather than fully exploiting the potential of new technologies, CBDCs may reinforce traditional structures and delay regulatory adaptation to financial innovation. From a political economy perspective, DeFi addresses many inefficiencies in the conventional financial system. In practice, blockchains and DeFi models are viable if the following conditions are met: (a) disintermediation is both technically and economically feasible, (b) transaction and data verification is essential for security and integrity, (c) multiple users need to share and access data efficiently, and (d) the business model relies on transactional trust and predictable outcomes.

The potential scope of financial services that meet these criteria is limited only by innovation. However, resistance from traditional financial institutions, outdated regulatory frameworks, and rapid technological advances present significant barriers. For FinTech to drive true disruption and social progress, greater collaboration is essential. Legal professionals must develop a deeper understanding of technology, while data scientists should expand their knowledge of financial regulations.

References

Accenture. (2021). *The economic impact of buy now, pay later in the US*. Retrieved October 12, 2024, from https://afterpay-newsroom.yourcreative.com.au/wp-content/uploads/2022/03/Economic-Impact-of-BNPL-in-the-US-vF.pdf

ACI Worldwide. (2025). *Payment gateways vs. payments orchestration: What is the difference and why it matters?* Retrieved February 5, 2025, from https://www.aciworldwide.com/blog/payment-gateways-vs-payments-orchestration-whats-the-difference-and-why-it-matters?utm_source=chatgpt.com

Affirm. (2023). *SEC Form 10-K*. Affirm Holdings, Inc. Retrieved November 11, 2024, from https://investors.affirm.com/static-files/5eb1286a-15c7-4014-a2ff-2ed2171843a9

Aggarwal, N., Goyal, D., Kumar, S., Nadarajah, S., & Pardasani, N. (2022). *Why pricing optimization can be a financial lifeline for FinTechs*. Boston Consulting Group. Retrieved December 1, 2024, from https://media-publications.bcg.com/Why-Pricing-Optimization-can-be-a-Financial-Lifeline-for-FinTechs.pdf

Akgiray, V. (2019). *The potential for blockchain technology in corporate governance*. OECD Corporate Governance Working Papers, No. 21. OECD Publishing. https://doi.org/10.1787/ef4eba4c-en

Alt, R., & Huch, S. (2022). *FinTech dictionary: Terminology for the digitalized financial world*. Springer.

Anderson, C. (2009). *Free: The future of a radical price*. Hyperion.

Anderson, M. H., & Jackson, R. (2004). Rent-to-own agreements: Purchases or rentals? *Journal of Applied Business Research (JABR), 20*(1). https://www.researchgate.net/publication/228874482_Rent-To-Own_Agreements_Purchases_Or_Rentals

T. Geçer and V. Akgiray, *The Financial Technology Revolution*, https://doi.org/10.1007/978-3-031-92048-6

Ankenbrand, T., Dietrich, A., Duss, C., & Wenli, R. (2016). *IFZ FinTech study 2016*. Lucerne University of Applied Sciences and Arts. Retrieved December 5, 2024, from https://www.hslu.ch/-/media/campus/common/files/dokumente/w/ifz/studien/FinTech-studie-160303.pdf/?sc_lang=de-ch

Arani, H. V., Pourakbar, M., Van der Laan, E., & De Koster, R. (2023). How do you charge for servicing: Per period or use? *European Journal of Operational Research, 304*(3). https://doi.org/10.1016/j.ejor.2022.05.002

Armaghan, M., Cakanyildirim, M., Frazelle, A., & Rajamani, D. (2023). *Buyout price optimization for the rent-to-own business*. SSRN. https://doi.org/10.2139/ssrn.4582364

Arnold, N., Claveres, G., & Frie, J. (2024). *Stepping up venture capital to finance innovation in Europe*. IMF Working Papers, WP/24/146. Retrieved November 21, 2024, from https://www.imf.org/-/media/Files/Publications/WP/2024/English/wpiea2024146-print-pdf.ashx

Axis Bank. (2023). *Integrated annual report 2023–24*. Retrieved December 11, 2024, from https://www.axisbank.com/annual-reports/2023-2024/pdf/annual-report-for-the-year-2023-2024.pdf

Azzuhri, A. A., Syarafina, A., Yoga, F. T., & Amalia, R. (2018). A creative, innovative, and solutive transportation for Indonesia with its setbacks and how to tackle them: A case study of the phenomenal GOJEK. *Review of Integrative Business and Economics Research, 7*(Suppl. 1), 59–67.

Barcellos, S. H., & Zamarro, G. (2021). Unbanked status and use of alternative financial services among minority populations. *Journal of Pension Economics & Finance, 20*(4), 468–481. https://doi.org/10.1017/S1474747219000052

Barclays. (2018). *POS finance consumer insights report*. Retrieved December 3, 2024, from https://www.barclayspartnerfinance.com/content/dam/bpf-core/BPF_CS_DID_ClientSurvey_029_AS.pdf

Basin, D., Sasse, R., & Toro-Pozo, J. (2021). Card brand mix-up attack: Bypassing the PIN in non-Visa cards by using them for Visa transactions. *USENIX Security Symposium Proceedings*. Retrieved October 25, 2024, from https://www.usenix.org/system/files/sec21-basin.pdf

Bavrova, O. S. (2021). The case of Tinkoff Bank as the pioneer of efficient neo-banking in Russia. *Proceedings of the International Scientific-Practical Conference ANPK-2021*. Retrieved December 23, 2024, from https://www.dvfu.ru/upload/medialibrary/41f/lsqohw24chr07uee7p6geis6xmqjz7tk/%D0%90%D0%9D%D0%9F%D0%9A-2021_.pdf#page=280

Bethlendi, A., & Szocs, A. (2022). How FinTech ecosystem changes with the entry of Big Tech companies. *Investment Management and Financial Innovations, 19*(3), 38–48. https://doi.org/10.21511/imfi.19(3).2022.04

BIS-Bank for International Settlements. (2019a). *Report on open banking and application programming interfaces*. Retrieved October 12, 2024, from https://www.bis.org/bcbs/publ/d486.pdf

BIS-Bank for International Settlements. (2019b). *BigTech in finance: Opportunities and risks*. BIS Annual Economic Report. Retrieved December 22, 2024, from https://www.bis.org/publ/arpdf/ar2019e3.pdf

BIS-Bank for International Settlements. (2022). *API standards for data-sharing (account aggregator) on open banking and application programming interfaces*. Retrieved October 21, 2024, from https://www.bis.org/publ/othp56.pdf

BIS-Bank for International Settlements. (2024). *Digitalisation of finance*. Retrieved December 15, 2024, from https://www.bis.org/bcbs/publ/d575.pdf

BKM. (2025). *History*. Retrieved February 5, 2025, from https://bkm.com.tr/en/about-bkm/bkm/history/

Block Inc. (2024). *Proxy statement: Notice of annual meeting of stockholders*. Block, Inc. Retrieved December 1, 2024, from https://s29.q4cdn.com/628966176/files/doc_financials/2024/ar/2024_Proxy_ARS.pdf

Boboev, S. (2024, March 13). *Deep dive: Embedded finance-Where everyday experiences meet financial solutions*. Finextra Blog. Retrieved December 19, 2024, from https://www.finextra.com/blogposting/25884/deep-dive-embedded-finance---where-everyday-experiences-meet-financial-solutions

Bonini, S., & Capizzi, V. (2019). *The role of venture capital in the entrepreneurial finance ecosystem: Future threats and opportunities*. SSRN Electronic Journal. https://doi.org/10.2139/ssrn.3315566

Bonus. (2025). *Bonus platformu*. Retrieved February 5, 2025, from https://www.bonus.com.tr/bonus-platformu

Brandl, B., & Hornuf, L. (2020). Where did FinTechs come from, and where do they go? The transformation of the financial industry in Germany after digitalization. *Frontiers in Artificial Intelligence, 3*(8). https://doi.org/10.3389/frai.2020.00008

Brown, G. G. L. (2021). *Early stage investments in FinTech ventures: Investors and their decision-making*. SSRN. https://doi.org/10.2139/ssrn.3868128

Campanella, F., Giudice, M., & Peruta, M. (2013). Informational approach of family spin-offs in the funding process of innovative projects: An empirical verification. *Journal of Innovation and Entrepreneurship, 2*(18). https://doi.org/10.1186/2192-5372-2-18

Carstens, A. (2020, March). Shaping the future of payments. *BIS Quarterly Review*. Retrieved September 9, 2024, from https://www.bis.org/publ/qtrpdf/r_qt2003e.pdf

CB Insights. (2019). *The top 20 reasons startups fail*. Retrieved October 11, 2024, from https://s3-us-west-2.amazonaws.com/cbi-content/research-reports/The-20-Reasons-Startups-Fail.pdf

CBRT-Central Bank of the Republic of Türkiye. (2024). *Press release on increasing FAST system transaction limits*. Retrieved September

12, 2024, from https://www.tcmb.gov.tr/wps/wcm/connect/EN/TCMB+EN/Main+Menu/Announcements/Press+Releases/2024/ANO2024-16

CCAF-Cambridge Centre for Alternative Finance. (2024). *The 2nd global crypto asset regulatory landscape study*. Retrieved December 21, 2024, from https://www.jbs.cam.ac.uk/wp-content/uploads/2024/10/2024-2nd-global-cryptoasset-regulatory-landscape-study.pdf

Checkout. (2025). *Open loop payments explained*. Retrieved February 5, 2025, from https://www.checkout.com/blog/open-loop-payment

Chen, L. (2023). Analysis of online platforms' free trial strategies for digital content subscription. *Journal of Theoretical and Applied Electronic Commerce Research, 18*(4), 2107–2124. https://doi.org/10.3390/jtaer18040106

Clark, D., & Camner, G. (2014). *A2A interoperability: Making mobile money schemes interoperate*. GSMA. Retrieved February 12, 2025, from https://www.gsma.com/solutions-and-impact/connectivity-for-good/mobile-for-development/wp-content/uploads/2014/03/A2A-interoperability_Online.pdf

Columbia Engineering. (2024). *What is financial technology (FinTech)? A beginner's guide*. Retrieved December 6, 2024, from https://bootcamp.cvn.columbia.edu/blog/what-is-FinTech/#1630507949220-e3b40a72-fb8b

Crisanto, J. C., Leuterio, C. B., Prenio, J., & Yong, J. (2024). *Regulating AI in the financial sector: Recent developments and main challenges*. FSI Insights, No. 63. Retrieved December 21, 2024, from https://www.bis.org/fsi/publ/insights63.pdf

Dealroom.co. (2022). *The rise of embedded finance: ABN AMRO Ventures and Dealroom.co*. Retrieved December 1, 2024, from https://dealroom.co/uploaded/2022/03/Dealroom-embedded-finance-v2-.pdf

Deloitte. (2021a). *Open banking: Unleashing the power of data and seizing new opportunities*. Retrieved September 14, 2024, from https://www2.deloitte.com/content/dam/Deloitte/in/Documents/financial-services/in-fs-open-banking-report-noexp.pdf

Deloitte. (2021b). *Banking as a service, explained: What it is, why it's important and how to play*. Retrieved November 1, 2024, from https://www2.deloitte.com/content/dam/Deloitte/cn/Documents/financial-services/deloitte-cn-fsi-importance-of-banking-as-a-service-en-211019.pdf

Deloitte. (2021c). *Value-based pricing: Aligning the cost and value of legal service*. Retrieved December 22, 2024, from https://www2.deloitte.com/content/dam/Deloitte/us/Documents/Tax/us-tax-value-based-pricing-aligning-the-cost-and-value-of-legal-services.pdf

Deloitte. (2021d). *Preparing for FinTech IPO*. Retrieved February 5, 2025, from https://www2.deloitte.com/content/dam/Deloitte/us/Documents/audit/us-fintech-ipos-keys-to-success.pdf

Deloitte. (2023). *Software pricing models: C-suite perspectives on consumption-based pricing and the elusive path to value*. Retrieved December 1, 2024, from https://www2.deloitte.com/content/dam/Deloitte/us/Documents/about-deloitte/us-deloitte-software-pricing-models.pdf

Dhar, V., & Stein, R. (2016). *FinTech platforms and strategy.* MIT Sloan Research Paper No. 5183-16. https://doi.org/10.2139/ssrn.2892098

ECB-European Central Bank. (2009). *Glossary of terms related to payment, clearing, and settlement systems.* Retrieved October 7, 2024, from https://www.ecb.europa.eu/pub/pdf/other/glossaryrelatedtopaymentclearingandsettlementsystemsen.pdf

ECB-European Central Bank. (2018). *Guide to assessments of fintech credit institution license applications.* Retrieved February 6, 2025, from https://www.bankingsupervision.europa.eu/ecb/pub/pdf/ssm.201803_guide_assessment_fintech_credit_inst_licensing.en.pdf

EC-European Commission. (2015). *Business innovation observatory, new business models: Freemium-zero marginal cost (Case study 49).* Retrieved November 1, 2024, from https://ec.europa.eu/docsroom/documents/13421/attachments/1/translations/en/renditions/native#:~:text=Freemium%20models%20with%20'zero'%20marginal,asset%20or%20a%20digital%20product

EC-European Commission. (2018). *Report from the Commission to the European Parliament and the Council on the implementation and impact of Directive 2009/110/EC, in particular on the application of prudential requirements for electronic money institutions.* Retrieved February 5, 2025, from https://eur-lex.europa.eu/resource.html?uri=cellar:ecb694ad-01bf-11e8-b8f5-01aa75ed71a1.0021.02/DOC_1&format=PDF

EMVCo. (2024a). *Overview of EMVCo.* Retrieved December 1, 2024, from https://www.emvco.com/about-us/overview-of-emvco/

EMVCo. (2024b). *What are EMV technologies?* Retrieved November 18, 2024, from https://www.emvco.com/emv-technologies/

Entrust. (2024). *Dynamic EMV solution: Everything you need for EMV data preparation and personalization.* Retrieved February 5, 2025, from https://www.entrust.com/sites/default/files/2024-08/dynamic-emv-solution-ds.pdf

Fasnacht, D. (2021). Banking 4.0: Digital ecosystems and super-apps. In K. Wendt (Ed.), *Theories of change: Sustainable finance* (pp. 15–30). Springer. https://doi.org/10.1007/978-3-030-52275-9_15

Feyen, E., Natarajan, H., & Saal, M. (2023). *FinTech and the future of finance: Market and policy implications.* World Bank. Retrieved October 22, 2024, from https://documents1.worldbank.org/curated/en/099450005162250110/pdf/P17300600228b70070914b0b5edf26e2f9f.pdf

Fiserv. (2020). *Card manufacturing digital brochure.* Retrieved February 6, 2025, from https://www.fiserv.com/content/dam/fiserv-ent/archive-files/final-files/card-manufacturing-digital-brochure.pdf

Fiserv. (2023a, March 6). *Understanding programmable payments.* Retrieved September 2, 2024, from https://www.fiserv.com/en/insights/articles-and-blogs/understanding-programmable-payments.html#:~:text=Programmable%20payments%20enable%20people%20to,ideal%20option%20for%20each%20transaction

Fiserv. (2023b). *SEC Form 10-K.* Retrieved December 1, 2024, from https://investors.fiserv.com/sec-filings/all-sec-filings/content/0000798354-24-000037/0000798354-24-000037.pdf

Fiserv. (2025). *Glossary.* Retrieved February 5, 2025, from https://merchants.fiserv.com/en-us/features/payments-101-glossary/#c

Floyd, C. (2024). New tech, old problem: The rise of virtual rent-to-own agreements. *Boston College Law Review, 65*(3), 763–832. https://bclawreview.bc.edu/articles/3123/files/6602bd596b4fc.pdf

Folwarski, M. (2020). Development of FinTech and BigTech companies and their expansion in the banking market. *Prace Naukowe Uniwersytetu Ekonomicznego we Wrocławiu, 64*(1), 44–54. https://doi.org/10.15611/pn.2020.1.04

FSB-Financial Stability Board. (2019). *FinTech and market structure in financial services: Market developments and potential financial stability implications.* Retrieved September 26, 2024, from https://www.fsb.org/wp-content/uploads/P140219.pdf

Gasser, U., Gassmann, O., Hens, T., Leifer, L., Puschmann, T., & Zhao, L. (2018). *Digital banking 2025.* Retrieved February 6, 2025, from https://www.fintech.uzh.ch/dam/jcr:2ef31105-1a60-43da-a657-8b140e47b3b4/Digital%20Banking%202025%20FINAL.pdf

Gcinisizwe, M., Jeník, I., & Zetterli, P. (2022). *Banking-as-a-service: How it can catalyze financial inclusion.* CGAP. Retrieved November 1, 2024, from https://www.cgap.org/research/reading-deck/banking-service-how-it-can-catalyze-financial-inclusion

Gemalto. (2014). *Annual report 2014.* Retrieved November 1, 2024, from https://www.bnains.org/archives/communiques/Gemalto/20150303_Annual_report_2014_Gemalto.pdf

Gimpel, H., Rau, D., & Röglinger, M. (2018). Understanding FinTech start-ups: A taxonomy of consumer-oriented service offerings. *Electronic Markets, 28*, 245–264. https://doi.org/10.1007/s12525-017-0275-0

GoTo. (2024). *Gojek at a glance.* Retrieved December 1, 2024, from https://www.gotocompany.com/en/products/gojek

Grant Thornton. (2019). *The FinTech lifecycle.* Retrieved February 5, 2025, from https://www.grantthornton.com.au/globalassets/1.-member-firms/australian-website/industry/financial-services/pdfs/gtal_2019_fintech_lifecycle.pdf

Guajardo, J. A. (2019). How do usage and payment behavior interact in rent-to-own business models? Evidence from developing economies. *Production and Operations Management, 28*(11), 2808–2822. https://doi.org/10.1111/poms.13067

Guerreiro, R., Cornachione, E. B., & Kassai, C. R. (2012). Determining the plus in cost-plus pricing: A time-based management approach. *Journal of Applied Management Accounting Research, 10*(1).

Haddad, C., & Hornuf, L. (2019). The emergence of the global FinTech market: Economic and technological determinants. *Small Business Economics, 53*, 81–105. https://doi.org/10.1007/s11187-018-9991-x

Hamari, J., Hanner, N., & Koivisto, J. (2020). Why pay a premium for freemium services? A study on perceived value, continued use, and purchase intentions in free-to-play games. *International Journal of Information Management, 51*. https://doi.org/10.1016/j.ijinfomgt.2019.102040

Harris, M., Davis, A., Adams, B., & Tijssen, J. (2022, September 12). *Embedded finance: What it takes to prosper in the new value chain*. Bain & Company, Inc. Retrieved September 6, 2024, from https://www.bain.com/insights/embedded-finance/

Hasan, Z. (2016). How Islamic is the diminishing musharakah model used for home financing? *Turkish Economic Review, 3*(3), 443–452.

Hasselwander, M. (2024). Digital platforms' growth strategies and the rise of super apps. *Heliyon, 10*(5). https://doi.org/10.1016/j.heliyon.2024.e25856

Hayashi, F., Markiewicz, Z., & Sullivan, R. J. (2016). *Chargebacks: Another payment card acceptance cost for merchants*. Federal Reserve Bank of Kansas City. https://doi.org/10.18651/RWP2016-01

Hensen, J., & Kötting, B. (2022). From open banking to embedded finance: The essential factors for a successful digital transformation. *Journal of Digital Banking, 6*(4), 308–318. https://doi.org/10.69554/SRCL3482

Hinterhuber, A. (2008). Customer value-based pricing strategies: Why companies resist. *Journal of Business Strategy, 29*(4), 41–50. https://doi.org/10.1108/02756660810887079

Holm, A. B., & Günzel-Jensen, F. (2017). Succeeding with freemium: Strategies for implementation. *Journal of Business Strategy, 38*(2). https://doi.org/10.1108/JBS-09-2016-0096

Holt, D., & Littlewood, D. (2014). *Reaching underbanked and unbanked in subsistence markets at the nexus of the formal and informal economy*. British Academy of Management Conference. Retrieved November 1, 2024, from https://centaur.reading.ac.uk/36921/1/BAM%2014%20Littlewood%20and%20Holt%20-%20Reading%20the%20unbanked%20and%20the%20underbanked%20in%20subsistence%20markets.pdf

Holvi. (2024). *Clear and simple pricing*. Retrieved December 14, 2024, from https://www.holvi.com/pricing/

Imenso Software. (2024). *Decoding FinTech business models: A comprehensive guide*. Retrieved February 6, 2025, from https://www.imensosoftware.com/blog/decoding-fintech-business-models-a-comprehensive-guide/

Interactive Brokers. (2023). *Annual report 2023*. Retrieved October 5, 2024, from https://investors.interactivebrokers.com/download/2023_IBG_AR.pdf

International Monetary Fund (IMF). (2022). *Global financial stability report*. Retrieved December 1, 2024, from https://www.elibrary.imf.org/downloadpdf/display/book/9798400205293/9798400205293.pdf

Janussek, M. (2022). Blessing or curse? The influence of neobrokers on the investment behavior of young investors. *Junior Management Science, 7*(5), 1375–1399. https://doi.org/10.5282/jums/v7i5pp1375-1399

J.P. Morgan. (2021). *The future of shopping: Digital wallets-Going everywhere your users go*. Retrieved November 1, 2024, from https://www.jpmorgan.com/content/dam/jpm/treasury-services/documents/google-digital-wallet.pdf

Juniper. (2023). *A2A payments: How A2A payments will reach critical mass in the UK and Europe*. Retrieved February 12, 2025, from https://25812054.fs1.hubspotusercontent-eu1.net/hubfs/25812054/Juniper%20Whitepaper%202023%20-%20A2A%20Payments%20Whitepaper.pdf

Kakao Corp. (2024). *Company presentation August 2024*. Retrieved September 24, 2024, from https://t1.kakaocdn.net/kakaocorp/admin/ir/results-announcement/5721.pdf

Kamal, I., Rizki, R. N., & Aulia, M. R. (2023). The enthusiasm for digital payment services and millennial user behavior in Indonesia. *International Journal of Professional Business Review, 8*(2). https://doi.org/10.26668/businessreview/2023.v8i2.923

Khasawneh, O., & Al-Bahsh, R. (2024). Why do people use mobile wallets? The case of fintech companies in Jordan. *Investment Management and Financial Innovations, 21*(2), 89–102. https://doi.org/10.21511/imfi.21(2).2024.07

Kim, S., Kwon, H. J., & Kim, H. (2023). Mobile banking service design attributes for the sustainability of internet-only banks: A case study of KakaoBank. *Sustainability, 15*(8), 6428. https://doi.org/10.3390/su15086428

Klarna Holding. (2023). *Annual report 2023*. Retrieved October 5, 2024, from https://assets.ctfassets.net/4pxjo1vaz7xk/4YoZpojIbRX6XbEdYPVUxg/6cddf386d1d29beca3c09f3d96c28104/Klarna_Holding_Annual_Report_2023.pdf

KoreFusion. (2021). *Embedded finance: This decade's largest creator of value*. KoreFusion LLC. Retrieved December 16, 2024, from https://44271344.fs1.hubspotusercontent-na1.net/hubfs/44271344/Descargables%20blog/KoreFusion%20-%20Embedded%20Finance%20-%20Whitepaper%20-%20Summer%202021%20final.pdf

Koroleva, E. (2022). *FinTech business models and their linkages with customers and founders* (Doctoral thesis, Tallinn University of Technology). https://digikogu.taltech.ee/en/Download/2560e67a-c6c2-42b1-8f3a-12a6a055fe3e

Kou, G., Akdeniz, O. Ö., Dinçer, H., & Yüksel, S. (2021). FinTech investments in European banks: A hybrid IT2 fuzzy multidimensional decision-making approach. *Financial Innovation, 7*(1), 1–28. https://doi.org/10.1186/s40854-021-00256-y

KPMG. (2017). *Value of FinTech.* Retrieved December 1, 2024, from https://assets.kpmg.com/content/dam/kpmg/uk/pdf/2017/10/value-of-fintech.pdf

KPMG. (2024). *Pulse of FinTech H2'23.* Retrieved February 5, 2025, from https://assets.kpmg.com/content/dam/kpmg/xx/pdf/2024/02/pulse-of-fintech-h2-2023.pdf

Lee, D. K. C., & Teo, E. G. S. (2015). *Emergence of FinTech and the Lasic principles.* SSRN Electronic Journal. https://doi.org/10.2139/ssrn.2668049

Levitin, A. J. (2017). Pandora's digital box: The promise and perils of digital wallets. *University of Pennsylvania Law Review, 166*, 305. https://doi.org/10.2139/ssrn.2899104

Lindström, C. W. J., Vishkaei, B. M., & De Giovanni, P. (2023). Subscription-based business models in the context of tech firms: Theory and applications. *International Journal of Industrial Engineering and Operations Management, 6*(3). https://doi.org/10.1108/IJIEOM-06-2023-0054

Liu, R., Wu, J., & Yu-Buck, G. F. (2021). The influence of mobile QR code payment on payment pleasure: Evidence from China. *International Journal of Bank Marketing, 39*, 337–356.

Lucas, J. D., & Lopes, E. (2024). *Defining a super app and analyzing it from an ecosystemic perspective.* https://doi.org/10.21203/rs.3.rs-4542297/v1

Maharani, S. (2023). The effect of user satisfaction and trust towards loyalty: A study on Starbucks card users. *Asian Journal of Research in Business and Management, 5*(3), 90–103. https://doi.org/10.55057/ajrbm.2023.5.3.8

Majumdar, S., & Pujari, V. (2022). Exploring usage of app banking in the UAE: A categorical regression analysis. *Journal of Financial Services Marketing, 27*, 177–189. https://doi.org/10.1057/s41264-021-00112-1

Malik, S., Kaur, M., & Kapoor, A. P. (2020). *Purchase now and pay later: Consumer preferences towards no cost EMIs in India.* First Pan IIT International Management Conference. https://doi.org/10.2139/ssrn.3743415

Markham, S. K. (2002). Moving technologies from lab to market. *Research-Technology Management, 45*, 31–42. https://doi.org/10.1080/08956308.2002.11671531

MasterCard. (2018). *Achieving business success in payment innovations.* Retrieved February 5, 2025, from https://www.mastercard.com/content/dam/mccom/gateway/documents/MC_WHITEPAPER_PAYMENT%20INOVATIONS-2018FINAL-GK.pdf

MasterCard. (2023). *SEC form 10-K*. Retrieved December 21, 2024, from https://s25.q4cdn.com/479285134/files/doc_financials/2023/AR/ma-12-31-2023-10-k-as-filed-with-exhibits.pdf

MasterCard. (2024). *Chargeback guide: Merchant edition*. Retrieved February 5, 2025, from https://www.mastercard.us/content/dam/public/mastercardcom/na/global-site/documents/chargeback-guide.pdf

McKinsey. (2022a). *Embedded finance: Who will lead the next payments revolution?* Retrieved December 2, 2024, from https://www.mckinsey.com/industries/financial-services/our-insights/embedded-finance-who-will-lead-the-next-payments-revolution

McKinsey. (2022b). *Sustaining payments growth: Winning models in emerging markets*. Retrieved December 17, 2024, from https://www.mckinsey.com/industries/financial-services/our-insights/sustaining-digital-payments-growth-winning-models-in-emerging-markets

McKinsey. (2023). *The 2023 global payments report: On the cusp of the next payments era*. Retrieved December 12, 2024, from https://www.mckinsey.com/industries/financial-services/our-insights

McKinsey. (2024a). *What is FinTech? McKinsey Explainers*. Retrieved December 22, 2024, from https://www.mckinsey.com/featured-insights/mckinsey-explainers/what-is-FinTech

McKinsey. (2024b). *The role of U.S. open banking in catalyzing the adoption of A2A payments*. Retrieved February 5, 2025, from https://www.mckinsey.com/industries/financial-services/our-insights/the-role-of-us-open-banking-in-catalyzing-the-adoption-of-a2a-payments

Mercer Capital. (2018). *How to value an early-stage FinTech company*. Retrieved November 1, 2024, from https://mercercapital.com/content/uploads/Mercer-Capital_How-to-Value-an-Early-Stage-FinTech-20181.pdf

Meyer, S., Uhr, C., & Johanning, L. (2021). *Private investors and the emergence of neobrokers: Does payment for order flow harm private investors?* WHU-Otto Beisheim School of Management. Retrieved October 2, 2024, from https://assets.traderepublic.com/assets/files/202111_study_private_investors_and_the_emergence_of_neo_brokers.pdf

Mizen, M. (2016). *Comparison of technologies for card printing applications*. 32nd International Conference on Digital Printing Technologies (NIP) Printing for Fabrication Conference.

Monzo. (2024). *Annual report 2024*. Retrieved November 21, 2024, from https://monzo.com/docs/monzo-annual-report-2024.pdf

Munifa, H. (2022). Customer relationship management strategy in Starbucks card optimization in the pandemic era. *International Journal for Educational and Vocational Studies*, *4*(1), 19–29. https://doi.org/10.29103/ijevs.v4i1.6817

Murthy, G., & Faz, X. (2021). *FinTech and financial inclusion: A funders' guide to greater impact*. Retrieved February 5, 2025, from https://www.cgap.org/sites/default/files/publications/2021_06_Focus_Note_FinTech_and_Financial_Inclusion_Funders_Guide.pdf

Nakamoto, S. (2008). *Bitcoin: A peer-to-peer electronic cash system (White Paper)*. Retrieved December 22, 2024, from https://Bitcoin.org/en/Bitcoin-paper

Neubert, M. (2017). International pricing strategies for born-global firms. *Central European Business Review, 6*(3), 41–50. https://doi.org/10.18267/j.cebr.185

Niu, X., & Zheng, Y. (2019). Credit card risk assessment based on machine learning. *Journal of Physics: Conference Series, 1213*, 1–7. https://doi.org/10.1088/1742-6596/1213/2/022015

Nordic APIs. (2018). *API strategy for open banking: Insights and case studies from leading open banking experts and API strategists*. Retrieved December 15, 2024, from https://nordicapis.com/wp-content/uploads/API-Strategy-for-Open-Banking-v2.2.pdf

Nubank. (2023). *SEC Form 20-F*. Retrieved December 16, 2024, from https://api.mziq.com/mzfilemanager/v2/d/59a081d2-0d63-4bb5-b786-4c07ae26bc74/8beb8998-9432-c707-c5a1-5432a393146a?origin=1

Nubank. (2024). *About Nu*. Retrieved September 11, 2024, from https://international.nubank.com.br/about/

OECD-Organization for Economic Co-operation and Development. (2024). *Regulatory approaches to artificial intelligence in finance*. OECD Artificial Intelligence Papers, No. 24. OECD Publishing. https://doi.org/10.1787/f1498c02-en

Oliver Wyman. (2018). *Breaking new ground in FinTech: A primer on revenue models that create value and build trust*. Retrieved December 19, 2024, from https://www.oliverwyman.com/content/dam/oliver-wyman/v2/publications/2018/october/Breaking%20New%20Ground%20in%20FinTech%20v2.pdf

Open Banking. (2024). *Open banking glossary*. Retrieved November 1, 2024, from https://www.openbanking.org.uk/glossary/#p

Osterwalder, A., Pigneur, Y., & Tucci, C. (2005). Clarifying business models: Origins, present, and future of the concept. *Communications of the Association for Information Systems, 16*(1), 1–25. https://doi.org/10.17705/1CAIS.01601

Ozili, P. K. (2022). Embedded finance: Assessing the benefits, use cases, challenges, and interest over time. *Journal of Internet and Digital Economics, 2*(2), 108–123. https://doi.org/10.1108/JIDE-05-2022-0014

Payfirma. (2016). *Payment processing 101: A merchant's guide to all things payments*. Retrieved December 21, 2024, from https://www.payfirma.com/wp-content/uploads/2016/01/Payfirma_ebook_PaymentProcessing101.pdf

Paypers. (2023). *Embedded finance and banking-as-a-service report 2023.* Retrieved February 6, 2025, from https://thepaypers.com/reports/embedded-finance-and-banking-as-a-service-report-2023/r1263680

PCI SSC-Payment Card Industry Security Standards Council. (2018). *Data security essentials for small merchants: Glossary of payment and information security terms.* Retrieved December 1, 2024, from https://listings.pcisecuritystandards.org/pdfs/Small_Merchant_Glossary_of_Payment_and_Information_Security_Terms.pdf

PCI SSC-Payment Card Industry Security Standards Council. (2022). *PCI DSS v4.0 quick reference guide: Understanding the payment card industry data security standard version 4.0.* Retrieved November 11, 2024, from https://www.pnc.com/content/dam/pnc-com/pdf/smallbusiness/Merchant%20Services/PCI_DSS_QuickRef_Guide.pdf

PCI SSC-Payment Card Industry Security Standards Council. (2024a). *Who we are.* Retrieved December 15, 2024, from https://www.pcisecuritystandards.org/about_us/

PCI SSC-Payment Card Industry Security Standards Council. (2024b). *Payment card industry data security standard version 4.0.1.* Retrieved November 1, 2024, from https://docs-prv.pcisecuritystandards.org/PCI%20DSS/Standard/PCI-DSS-v4_0_1.pdf

Petrovska, I., Šerovska, G., & Kovačevski, D. (2019). Value-based pricing strategies in retail: Effective or not? *Journal of Innovative Business and Management, 9*(2). Retrieved December 11, 2024, from https://journal.doba.si/ojs/index.php/jimb/article/view/48/63

Pramani, R., & Iyer, S. V. (2023). Adoption of payments banks: A grounded theory approach. *Journal of Financial Services Marketing, 28*, 43–57. https://doi.org/10.1057/s41264-021-00133-w

Pujol, N. (2010). *Freemium: Attributes of an emerging business model.* https://doi.org/10.2139/ssrn.1718663

Puzhakkal, R., & Sivansankaran, S. (2024). FinTech: A steppingstone towards financial inclusion. *Journal of Business Management and Information Systems, 11*(6). https://doi.org/10.48001/jbmis.2024.si1006

PwC-PricewaterhouseCoopers. (2019). *Pricing innovation in banking: The next frontier.* Retrieved December 4, 2024, from https://www.pwc.in/assets/pdfs/research-insights/2019/pricing-innovation-in-banking.pdf

Revenue Management Labs. (2024). *A complete guide: Driving business success with pricing in line with the market.* Retrieved December 10, 2024, from https://revenueml.com/wp-content/uploads/2024/05/Competitive-Pricing.pdf

Reynolds, F. (2017). *Open banking: A consumer perspective.* Retrieved November 21, 2024, from https://www.openbanking.org.uk/wp-content/uploads/2021/04/Open-Banking-A-Consumer-Perspective.pdf

Robinhood. (2023). *SEC Form 10-K*. Retrieved November 1, 2024, from https://d18rn0p25nwr6d.cloudfront.net/CIK-0001783879/78bc4a0f-d3b2-452e-8ac1-27f366e46bd4.pdf

Rubini, A. (2024). Financial technology made easy. *Walter de Gruyter GmbH*. https://doi.org/10.1515/9781547401055

Saini, A. K. (2018). FinTech revolution and future of banking and financial institutions: Quantitative investigation. *Psychology and Education, 55*(1), 428–436. https://doi.org/10.48047/pne.2018.55.1.53

Schueffel, P. (2017). *The concise FinTech compendium*. Retrieved November 21, 2024, from https://www.researchgate.net/publication/322819310_The_Concise_FinTech_Compendium

Sezzle. (2023). *2023 annual report*. Retrieved December 4, 2024, from https://assets.ctfassets.net/6d085vujy22q/3FbsrsHyvQyruhVkqN2gbZ/27d7d83fcdd927f495d1ef7d39201750/2023_Annual_Report.pdf

Sifted. (2022). *Embedded finance: The new face of banking*. Retrieved February 5, 2025, from https://sifted.eu/intelligence/reports/embedded-finance

Smeureanu, I., Ruxanda, G., & Badea, L. M. (2013). Customer segmentation in private banking sector using machine learning techniques. *Journal of Business Economics and Management, 14*(5), 923–939. https://doi.org/10.3846/16111699.2012.749807

Solarisbank. (2023). *Sustainability report 2023*. Retrieved November 3, 2024, from https://www.solarisgroup.com/content/solaris-npb-report-2023.pdf

Solarisbank. (2024). *Discover our services*. Retrieved December 23, 2024, from https://www.solarisgroup.com/en/services/

Starbucks. (2023). *Starbucks fiscal 2023 annual report*. Retrieved December 5, 2024, from https://s203.q4cdn.com/326826266/files/doc_financials/2024/ar/fy23-annual-report.pdf

Stripe. (2024a). *Klarna: An in-depth guide*. Retrieved November 11, 2024, from https://stripe.com/resources/more/klarna-an-in-depth-guide

Stripe. (2024b). *What is payment orchestration? What businesses need to know*. Retrieved February 5, 2025, from https://stripe.com/gb/resources/more/what-is-payment-orchestration-what-businesses-need-to-know?utm_source=chatgpt.com

Tanda, A., & Schena, C. M. (2019). *FinTech, BigTech and banks*. https://doi.org/10.1007/978-3-030-22426-4

Thales. (2023). *Integrated report 2023–2024*. Retrieved December 1, 2024, from https://www2.thalesgroup.com/2024/rapport-integre/files/thales-integrated-report-2023-en.pdf

Thales. (2024a). *Digital identity and security*. Retrieved November 10, 2024, from https://www.thalesgroup.com/en/markets/digital-identity-and-security

Thales. (2024b). *What do hardware security modules do?* Retrieved February 5, 2025, from https://cpl.thalesgroup.com/encryption/hardware-security-modules

Tijssen, J., & Garner, R. (2021). *Buy now, pay later in the UK*. Bain & Company, Inc. Retrieved December 17, 2024, from https://www.bain.com/globalassets/noindex/2021/bain_report_buy_now_pay_later-in-the-uk.pdf

Tinkoff. (2024). *Online financial ecosystem centred around the needs of its customers*. Retrieved November 8, 2024, from https://tinkoff-group.com/company-info/summary/

Tobin, J. (1985). Financial innovation and deregulation in perspective. *Bank of Japan Monetary & Economic Studies, 19*, 20–21. Retrieved December 22, 2024, from https://www.imes.boj.or.jp/research/papers/english/me3-2-3.pdf

Turi, A. N. (2023). *Financial technologies and DeFi: A revisit to the digital finance revolution*. https://doi.org/10.1007/978-3-031-17998-3

United Nations (UN). (2023). *FinTech and digital finance for financial inclusion: Policy brief*. Retrieved December 5, 2024, from https://www.un.org/sites/un2.un.org/files/FinTech4_14_march_2023.pdf

U.S. Faster Payments Council (US FPC). (2022). *QR codes for faster payments*. Retrieved December 6, 2024, from https://fasterpaymentscouncil.org/userfiles/2080/files/QR%20Code%20White%20Paper_07-25-2022_Final(2).pdf

U.S. Payments Forum. (2018). *Mobile and digital wallets: U.S. landscape and strategic considerations for merchants and financial institutions*. Retrieved December 1, 2024, from https://www.uspaymentsforum.org/wp-content/uploads/2018/01/Mobile-Digital-Wallets-WP-FINAL-January-2018.pdf

Varma, P., Nijjer, S., Sood, K. S., Grima, S., & Rupeika-Apoga, R. (2022). Thematic analysis of financial technology (FinTech) influence on banking industry. *Risks, 10*(10), 186. https://doi.org/10.3390/risks10100186

Visa. (2022). *Buy now, pay later: A threat or an opportunity?* Visa Consulting & Analytics. Retrieved December 21, 2024, from https://www.visa.co.uk/content/dam/VCOM/regional/ve/unitedkingdom/PDF/vca/uk-vca-how-can-you-capitalise-on-bnpl-innovation-and-growth.pdf

Visa. (2023a). *Four ways open-loop systems make transit better for everyone*. Retrieved February 5, 2025, from https://usa.visa.com/visa-everywhere/blog/bdp/2023/04/17/four-ways-open-1681749375512.html

Visa. (2023b). *Embedded finance: What are the emerging opportunities in this new value chain?* Visa Consulting & Analytics. Retrieved October 11, 2024, from https://corporate.visa.com/content/dam/VCOM/global/services/documents/vca-embedded-finance-emerging-trends.pdf

Visa. (2024a). *Annual report 2024*. Retrieved February 5, 2025, from https://s29.q4cdn.com/385744025/files/doc_downloads/2024/Visa-Fiscal-2024-Annual-Report.pdf

Visa. (2024b). *Digital wallets in Visa's ecosystem: Policies & requirements.* Retrieved December 12, 2024, from https://usa.visa.com/content/dam/VCOM/global/support-legal/documents/digital-wallet-guide-october-2024.pdf

Wang, L. (2023). FinTech: Digital transformation in finance. *Advances in Economics, Management and Political Sciences, 40*, 22–27. https://doi.org/10.54254/2754-1169/40/20231983

Wehrs, D., & Parker, C. (2020). *The startup pricing journey: How to efficiently monetize products and services.* Bessemer Venture Partners. Retrieved November 13, 2024, from https://www.bvp.com/assets/uploads/2021/05/the-startup-pricing-journey.pdf

Weinmayr, J., Rappold, D., Tricoire, J., Bradley, M., & Bercot, J. (2020). *The ultimate guide to startup metrics: What to track, when and why.* Speedinvest Pirates. Retrieved November 14, 2024, from https://cdn.prod.website-files.com/622d3d1f98d09af01f927fb9/640f4a4993d5dabfc06797fb_speedinvest-pirates-the-ultimate-guide-to-startup-metrics.pdf

WhiteSight. (2023). *Apple at the forefront of the embedded finance revolution.* Retrieved December 15, 2024, from https://whitesight.net/wp-content/uploads/2023/06/Apples-Embedded-Finance-Playbook-Product-Preview.pdf

Wise. (2024). *Annual report and accounts.* Retrieved December 21, 2024, from https://wise.com/imaginary-v2/images/3f1628373b212ca54c1ac73c68d69b72-WISE-2024-Annual-Report-and-Accounts.pdf

World Bank Group. (2021). *The use of quick-response codes in payments.* Retrieved November 18, 2024, from https://fastpayments.worldbank.org/sites/default/files/2021-10/QR_Codes_in_Payments_Final.pdf

World Economic Forum (WEF). (2015). *The future of financial services.* Retrieved October 12, 2024, from https://www3.weforum.org/docs/WEF_The_future__of_financial_services.pdf

Worldpay. (2023). *The global payments report 2023.* Retrieved November 1, 2024, from https://www.fisglobal.com/en/global-payments-report

WorldRemit. (2021). *WorldRemit Group Limited annual report and financial statements for the year ended 31 December 2021.* Retrieved October 21, 2024, from https://assets.ctfassets.net/sb7j5o4oxtgv/1px52RScz6YPAHXo6S3UkG/dd0813b08308a97ea50b57a7b6880d6c/WR_Group_Limited_Stat_FY21_ISA_accounts.docx.pdf

World Savings and Retail Banking Institute (WSBI) & European Savings and Retail Banking Group (ESBG). (2022, July 14). *Number of unbanked adult EU citizens more than halved in the last four years.* Retrieved September 28, 2024, from https://www.wsbi-esbg.org/number-of-unbanked-adult-eu-citizens-more-than-halved-in-the-last-four-years/

Wu, S., & Pavlou, P. (2019). On the optimal fixed-up-to pricing for information services. *Journal of the Association for Information Systems, 20*(10). https://doi.org/10.17705/1jais.00574

Yan, B. (2023). An investigation on Klarna financial technology FinTech. *Advances in Economics, Management and Political Sciences, 64*, 134–142. https://doi.org/10.54254/2754-1169/64/20231515

Ye, S. (2022). The rise of superapps in emerging countries. *Advances in Economics, Business and Management Research.* https://doi.org/10.2991/978-94-6463-098-5_207

Index

T. Geçer and V. Akgiray, *The Financial Technology Revolution*, https://doi.org/10.1007/978-3-031-92048-6

FSC
www.fsc.org
MIX
Papier | Fördert
gute Waldnutzung
FSC® C083411

Kolibri 360 GmbH
Ferdinand-Jühlke-Straße 7
99095 Erfurt, Deutschland
produktsicherheit@kolibri360.de